EASY GUITAR WITH NOTES & TAB

Classical Melodies

ISBN 978-1-4950-6292-6

HAL•LEONARD® CORPORATION

7777 W. BLUEMOUND RD. P.O. BOX 13819 MILWAUKEE, WI 53213

In Australia Contact:
Hal Leonard Australia Pty. Ltd.
4 Lentara Court
Cheltenham, Victoria, 3192 Australia
Email: ausadmin@halleonard.com.au

Visit Hal Leonard Online at
www.halleonard.com

STRUM AND PICK PATTERNS

This chart contains the suggested strum and pick patterns that are referred to by number at the beginning
of each song in this book. The symbols ⊓ and ∨ in the strum patterns refer to down and up strokes, respectively.
The letters in the pick patterns indicate which right-hand fingers play which strings.

p = thumb
i = index finger
m = middle finger
a = ring finger

For example; Pick Pattern 2
is played: thumb - index - middle - ring

Strum Patterns   ## Pick Patterns

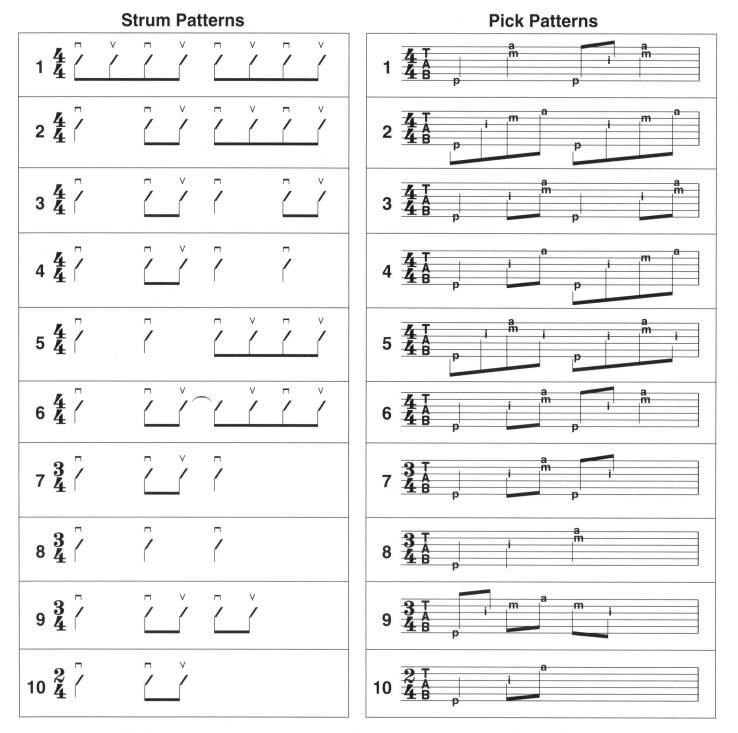

You can use the 3/4 Strum and Pick Patterns in songs written in compound meter (6/8, 9/8, 12/8, etc.).
For example, you can accompany a song in 6/8 by playing the 3/4 pattern twice in each measure.
The 4/4 Strum and Pick Patterns can be used for songs written in cut time (¢) by doubling the note
time values in the patterns. Each pattern would therefore last two measures in cut time.

Arioso

from CANTATA NO. 156

By Johann Sebastian Bach

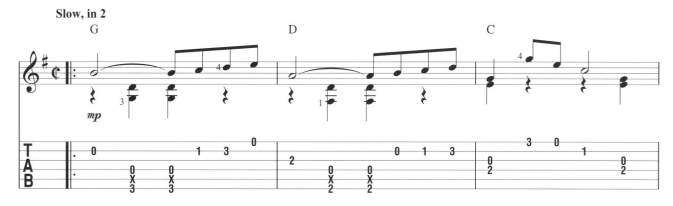

Strum Pattern: 4
Pick Pattern: 4

Slow, in 2

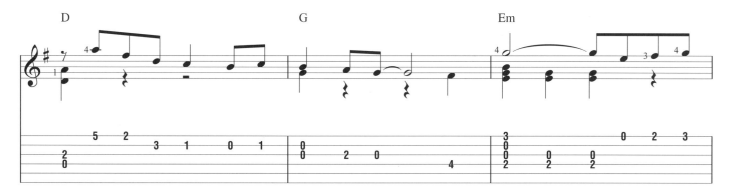

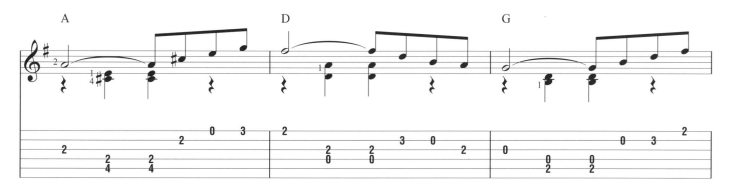

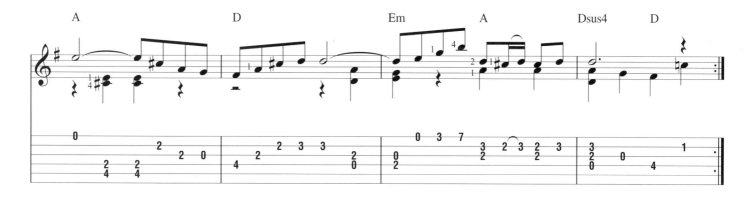

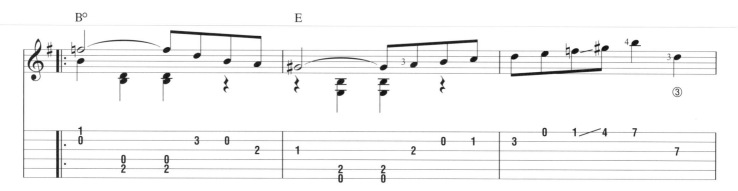

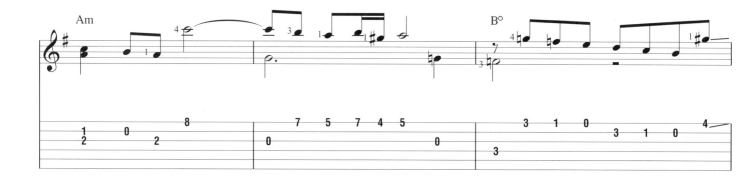

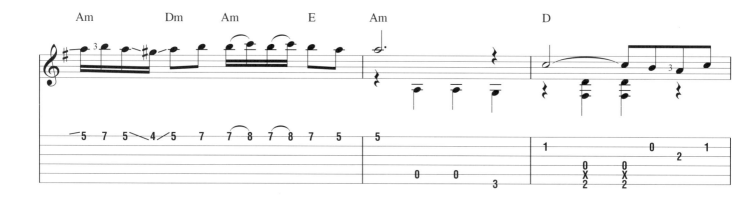

4

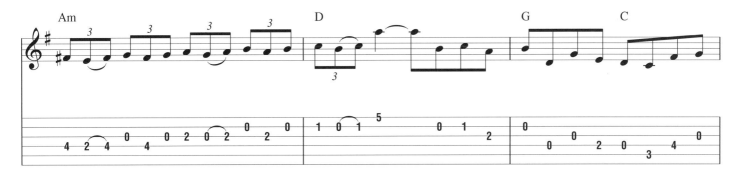

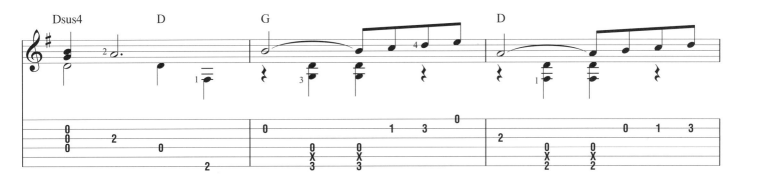

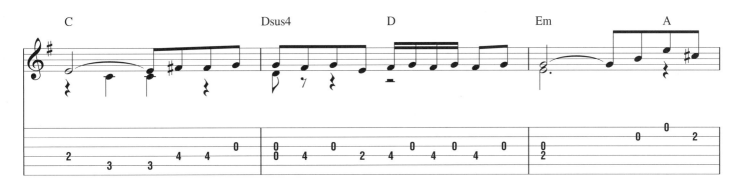

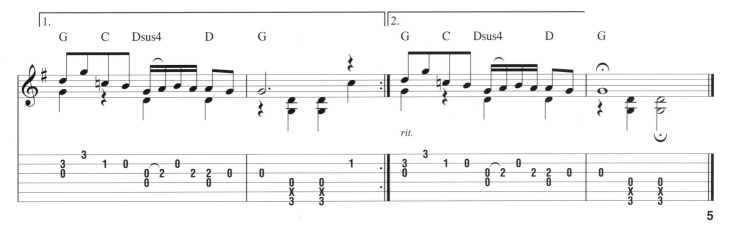

Air on the G String

from ORCHESTRAL SUITE NO. 3

By Johann Sebastian Bach

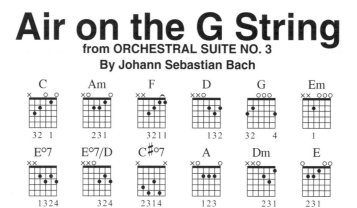

Strum Pattern: 3
Pick Pattern: 3

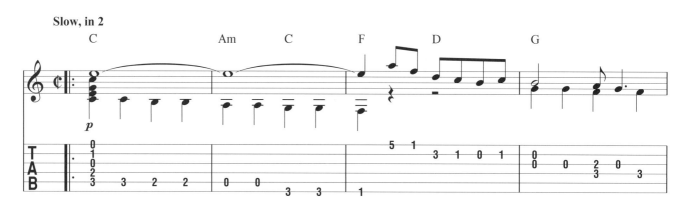

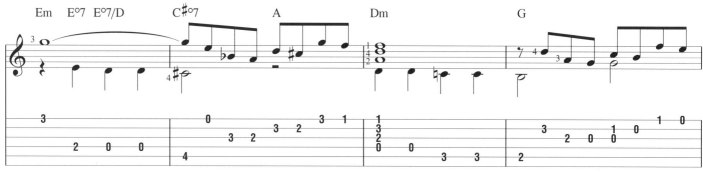

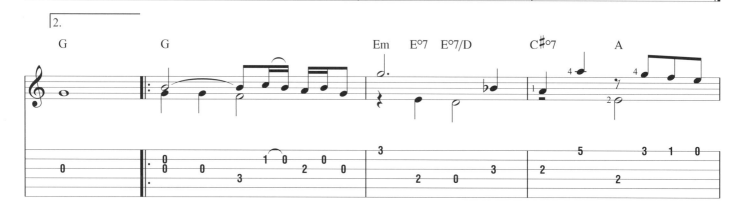

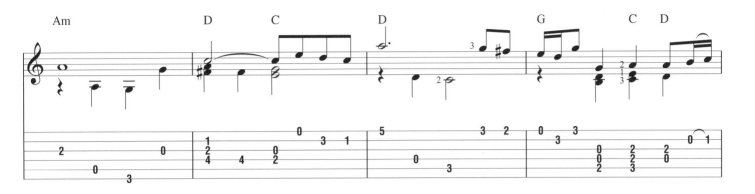

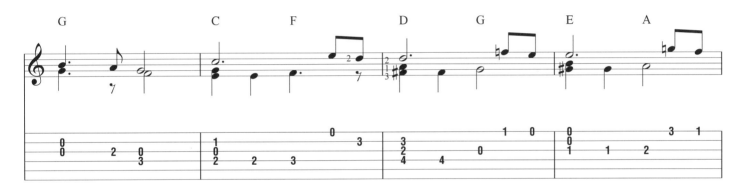

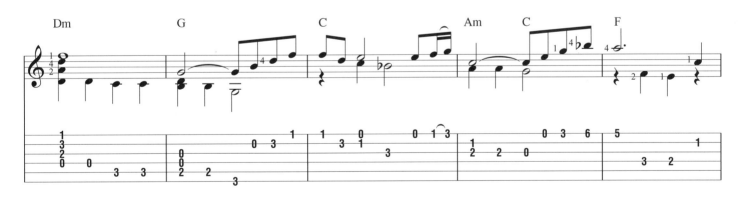

Blue Danube Waltz

By Johann Strauss, Jr.

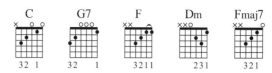

Strum Pattern: 7, 8
Pick Pattern: 8

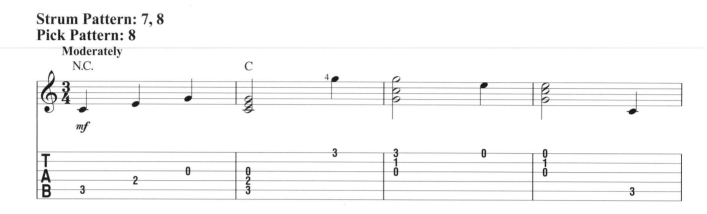

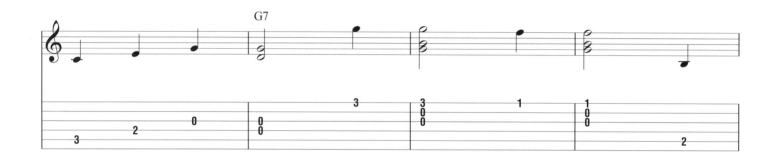

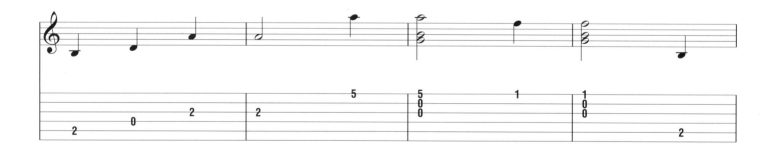

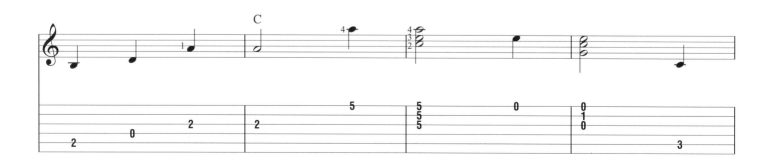

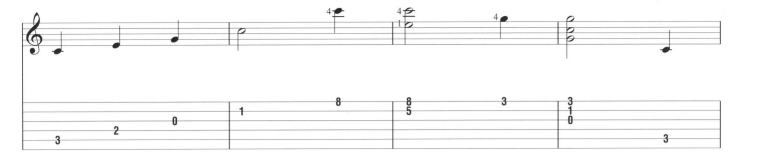

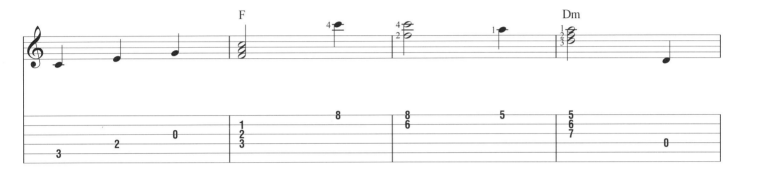

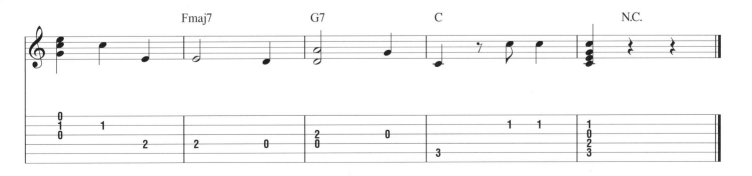

Can Can

from ORPHEUS IN THE UNDERWORLD

By Jacques Offenbach

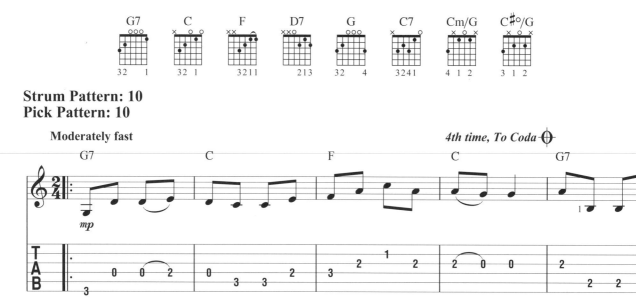

Strum Pattern: 10
Pick Pattern: 10

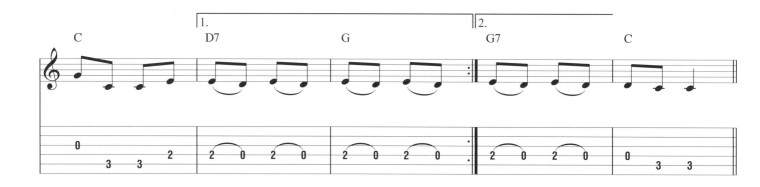

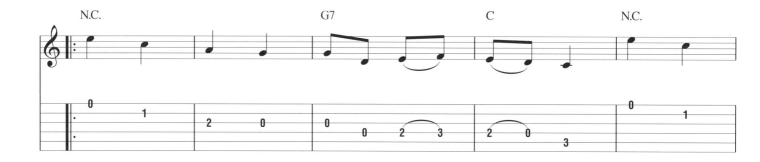

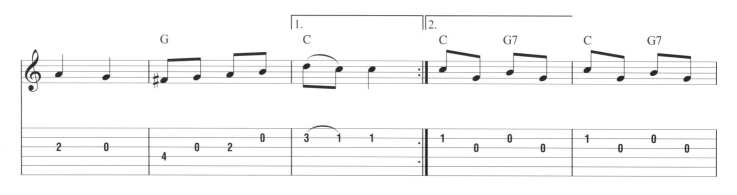

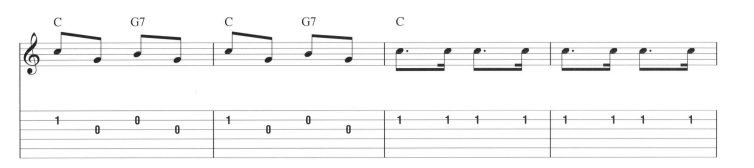

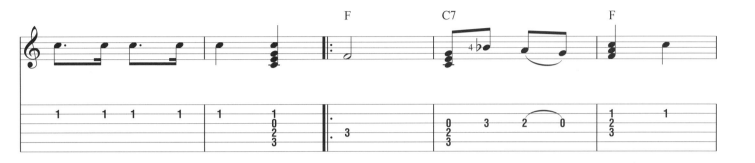

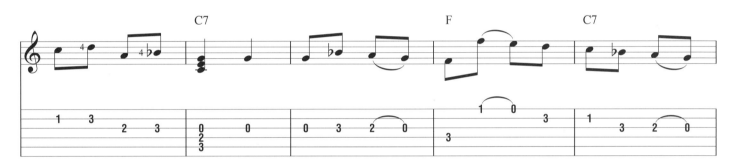

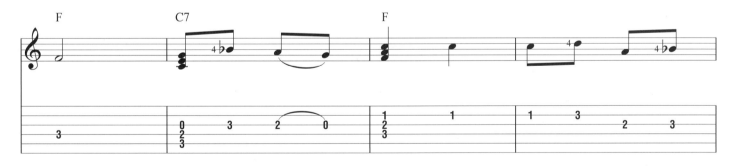

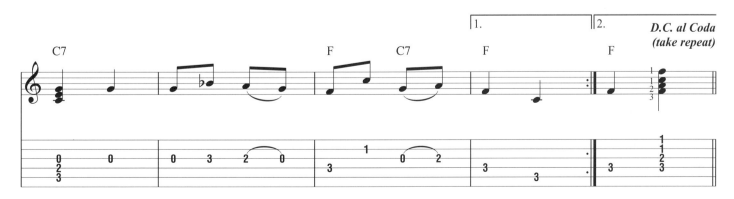

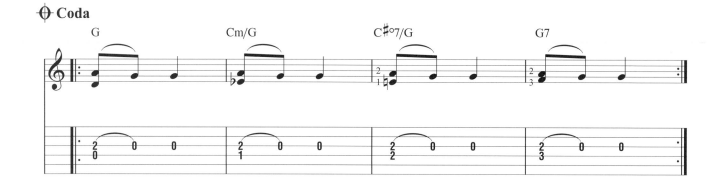

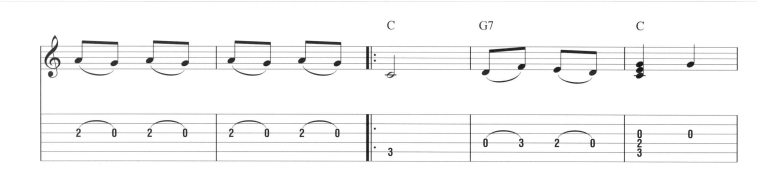

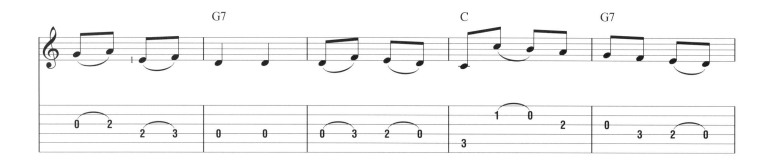

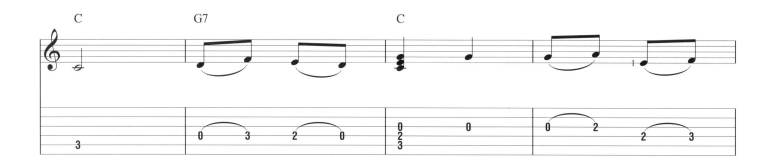

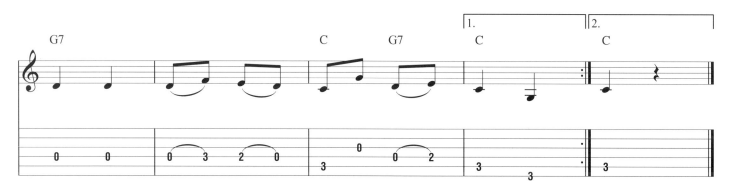

Für Elise

By Ludwig van Beethoven

Strum Pattern: 7, 9
Pick Pattern: 7, 9

Moderately slow

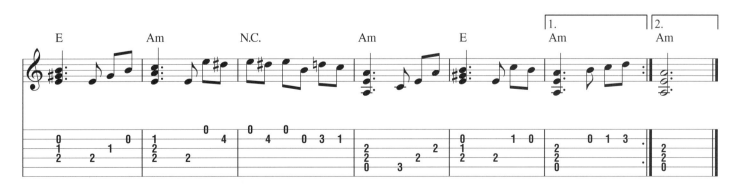

Dance of the Sugar Plum Fairy

from THE NUTCRACKER
By Pyotr Il'yich Tchaikovsky

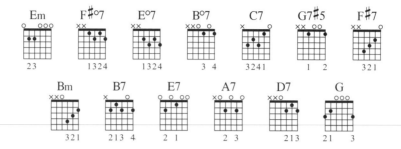

Strum Pattern: 4
Pick Pattern: 1
Moderately

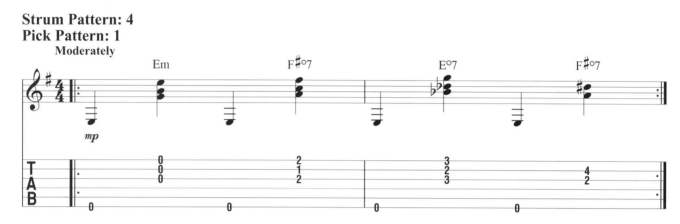

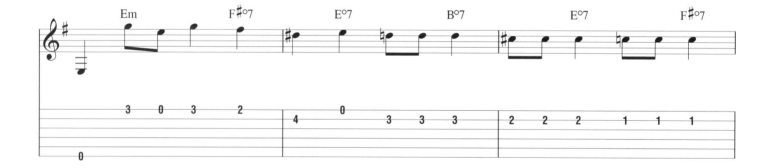

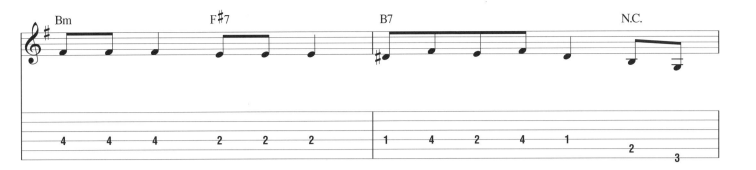

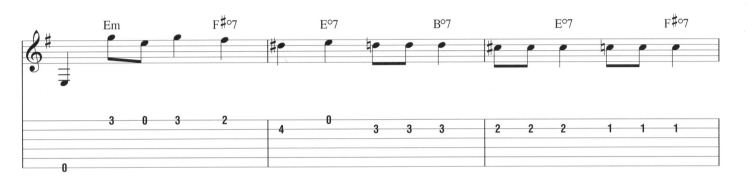

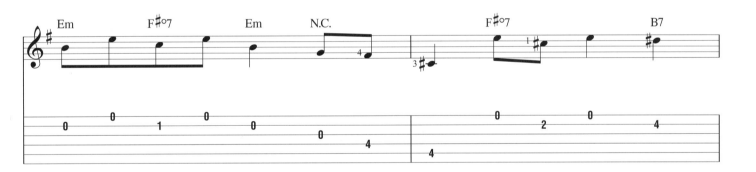

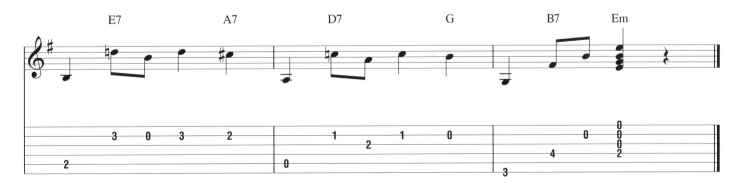

Emperor Waltz

By Johann Strauss, Jr.

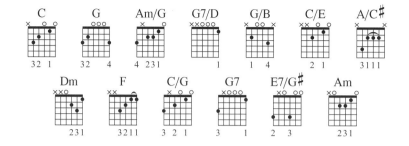

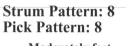

Strum Pattern: 8
Pick Pattern: 8

Moderately fast

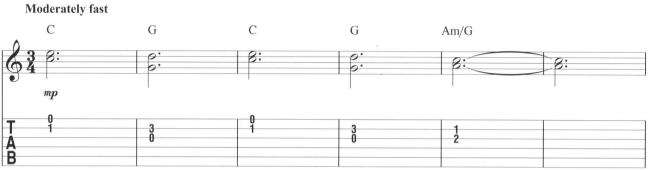

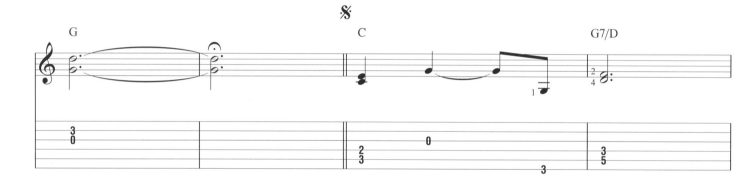

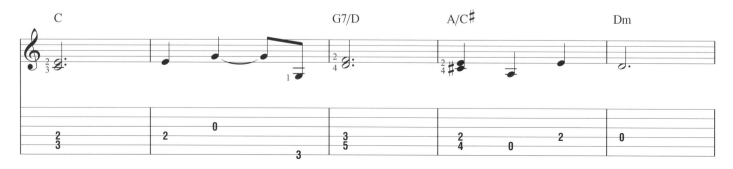

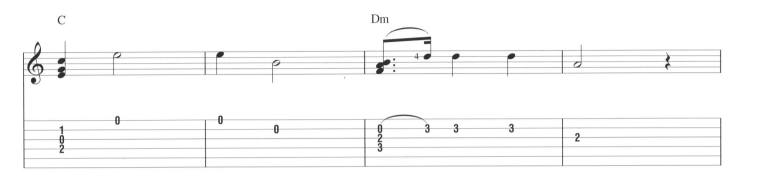

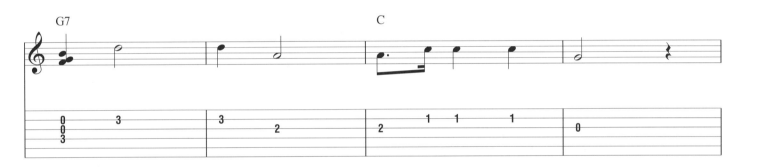

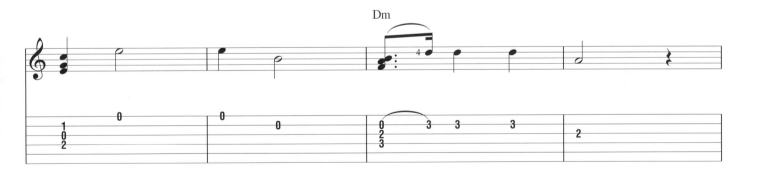

D.S. al Fine

Fugue in G Minor ("Little")

By Johann Sebastian Bach

Strum Pattern: 3
Pick Pattern: 5

*Arranged in D minor for playability.

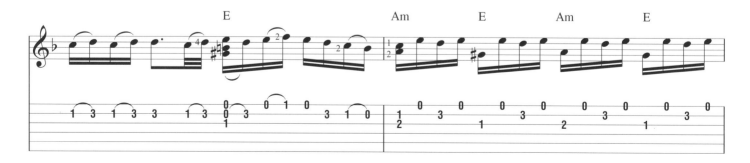

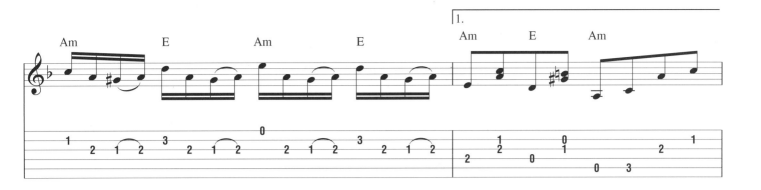

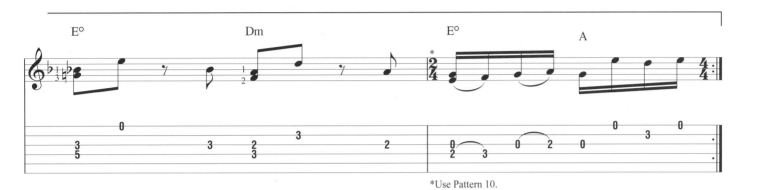

*Use Pattern 10.

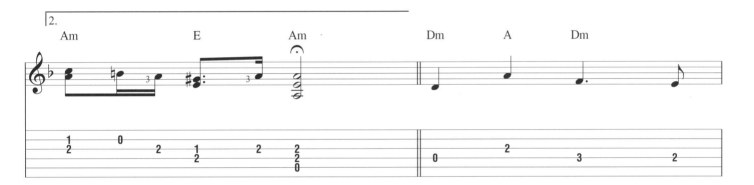

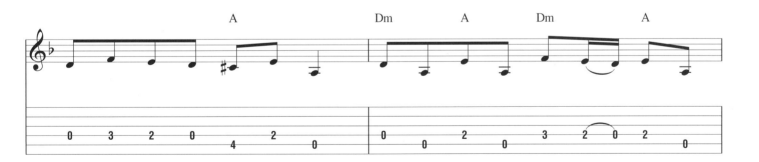

Gypsy Rondo

By Franz Joseph Haydn

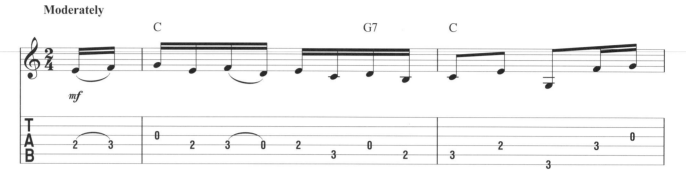

Strum Pattern: 10
Pick Pattern: 10

Moderately

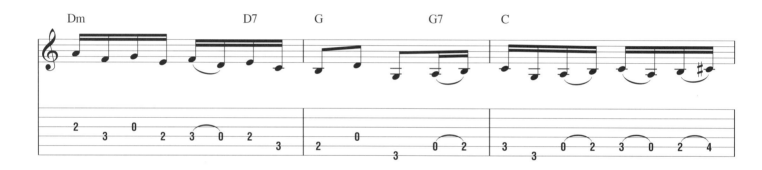

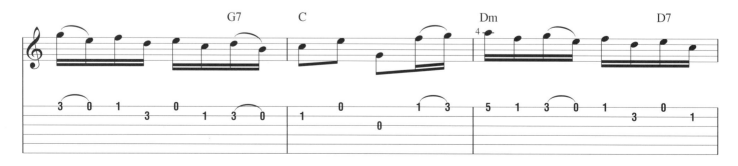

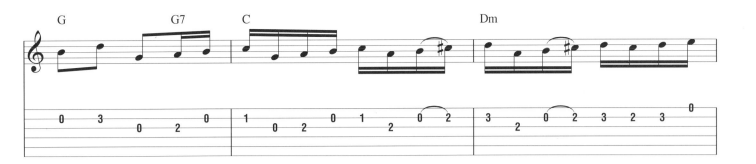

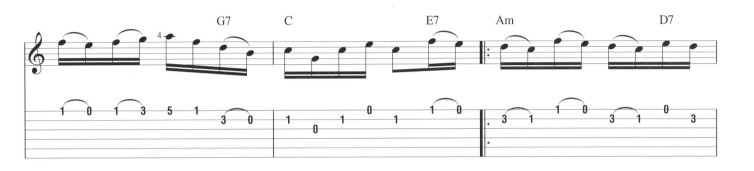

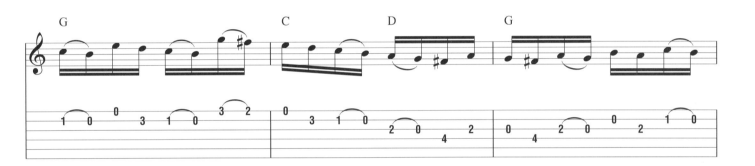

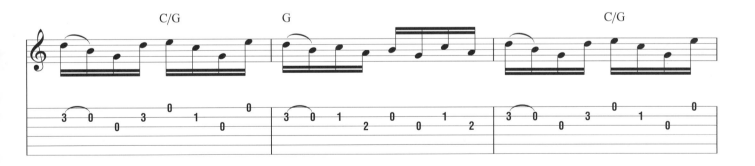

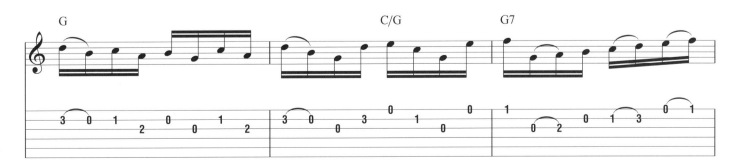

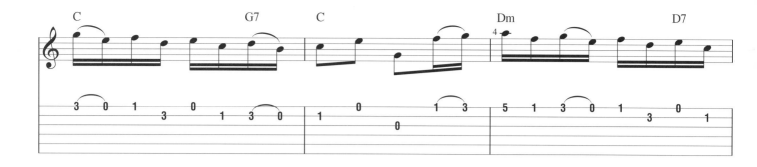

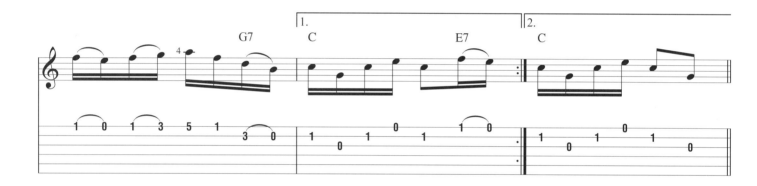

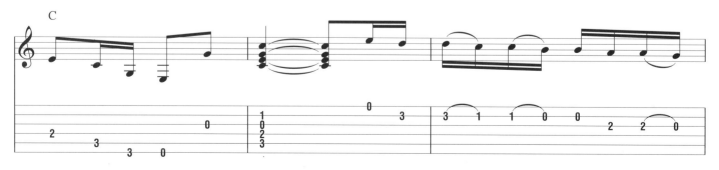

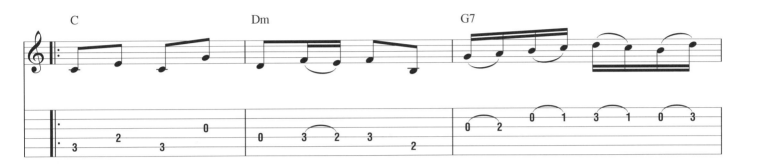

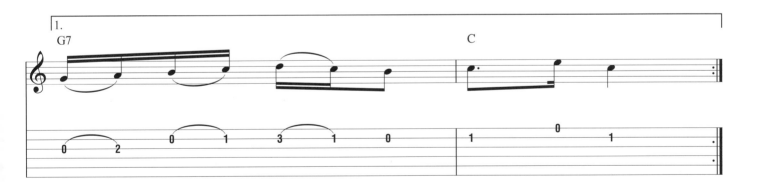

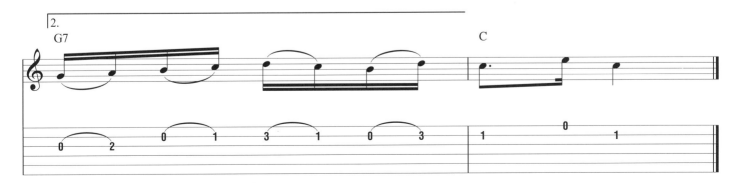

The Happy Farmer

By Robert Schumann

Strum Pattern: 3
Pick Pattern: 5

Moderately fast

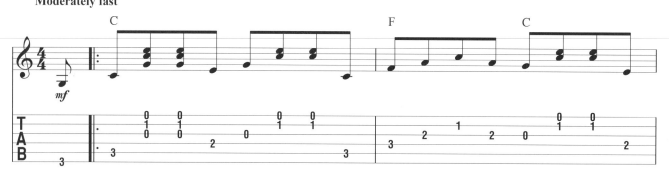

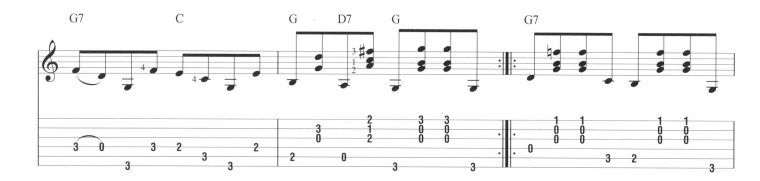

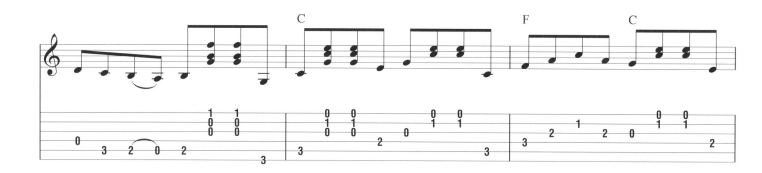

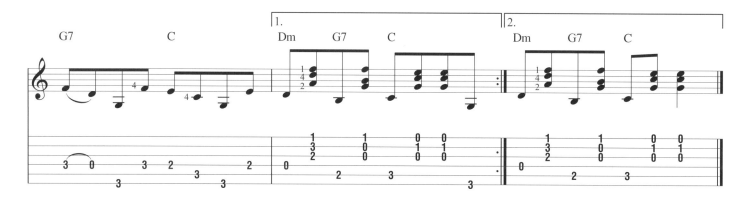

La donna è mobile

from RIGOLETTO

By Giuseppe Verdi

Strum Pattern: 8
Pick Pattern: 8

Verse
Moderately fast

1. La Don - n è Mo - bi - le qual piu ma ven - to

mu - ta - d'ac - cen - to e di pen - sie - ro.

Chorus

La - Don - na è mo - bil qual ___ piu ma al ven - to _____

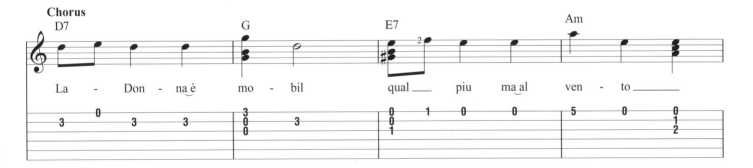

mu - ta d'ac - cen - to e ___ di pen - sier.

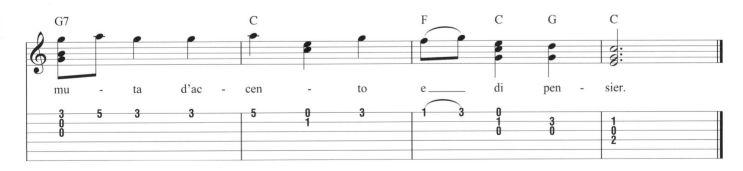

Additional Lyrics

2. Sempre un a Mobile qual piu ma al vento
   Mu ta d'accento e di pensiero.

Humoresque

By Antonín Dvořák

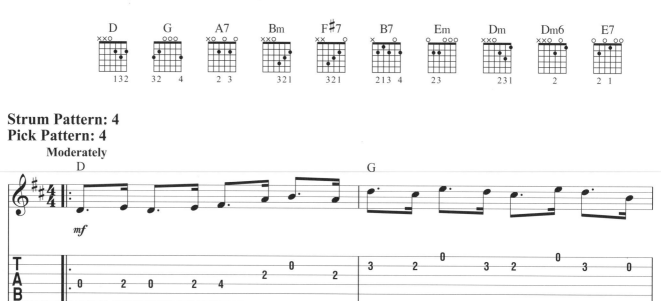

Strum Pattern: 4
Pick Pattern: 4

Moderately

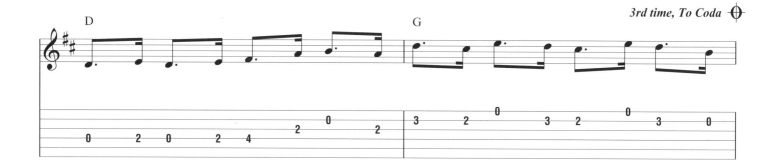

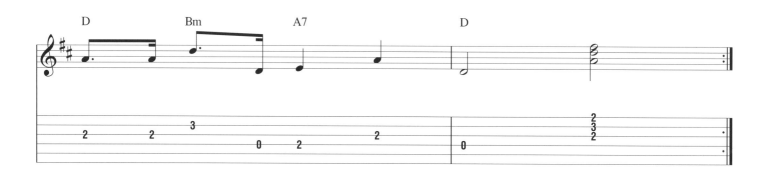

D.C. al Coda

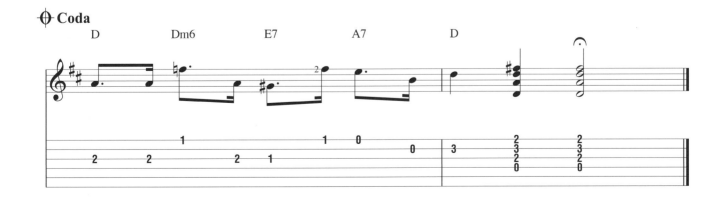

In the Hall of the Mountain King

from PEER GYNT

By Edvard Grieg

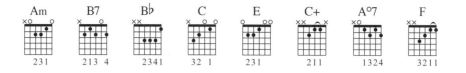

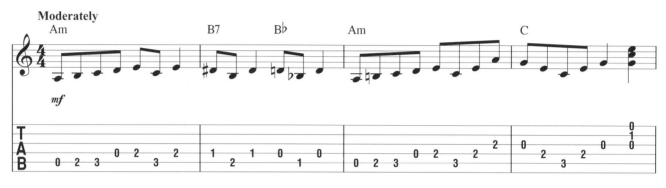

Strum Pattern: 3
Pick Pattern: 4

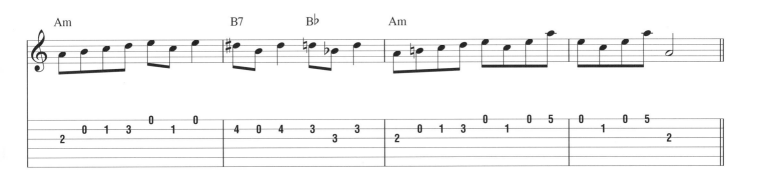

Lullaby
(Cradle Song)

By Johannes Brahms

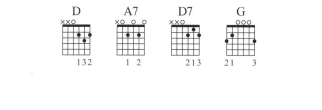

Strum Pattern: 7
Pick Pattern: 7

Minuet

from THE STRING QUINTET IN E MAJOR, OP. 11, NO. 5

By Luigi Boccherini

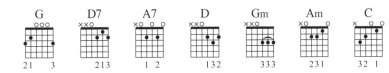

Strum Pattern: 8
Pick Pattern: 8

Moderately

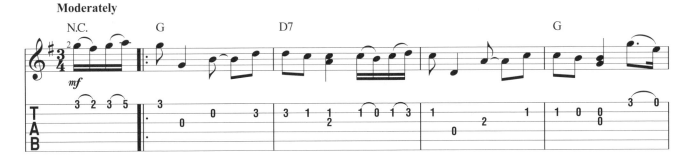

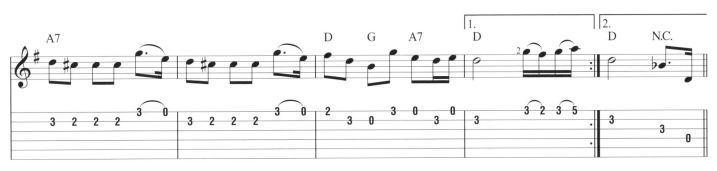

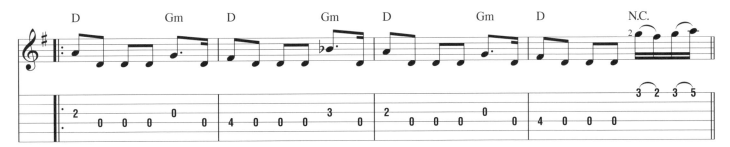

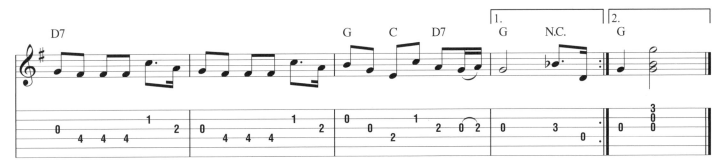

March (Tannhäuser)

By Richard Wagner

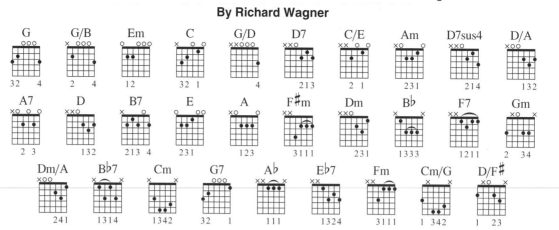

Strum Pattern: 4
Pick Pattern: 4

Moderately slow, in 2

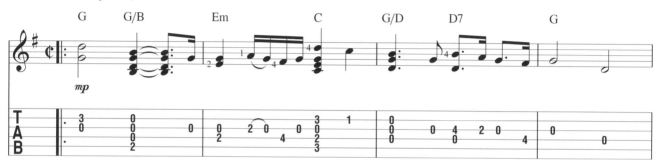

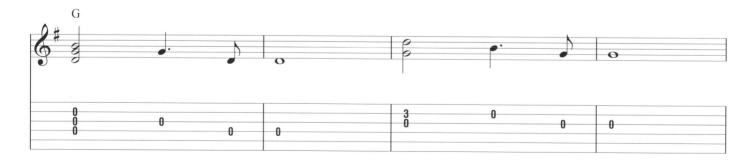

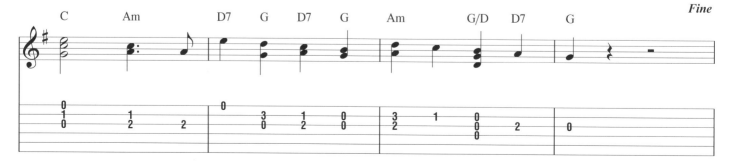

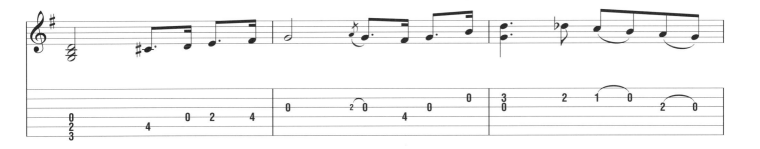

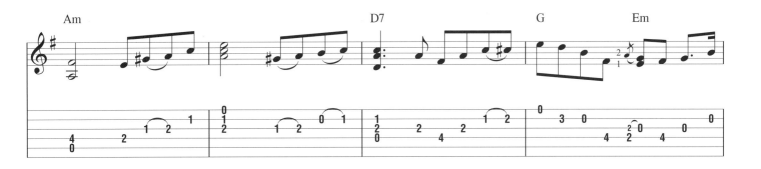

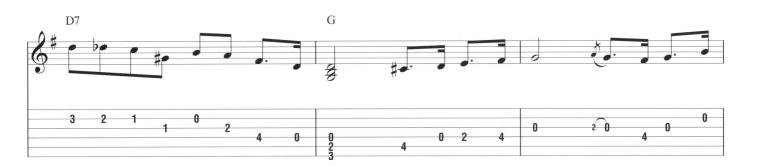

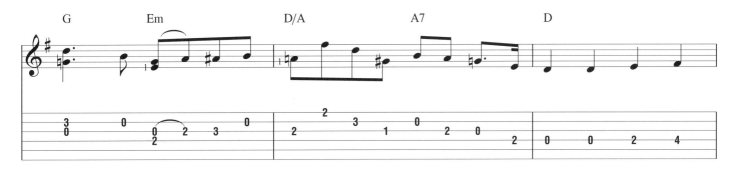

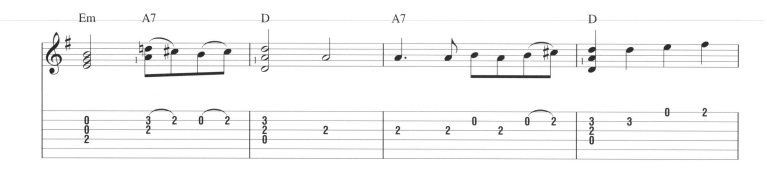

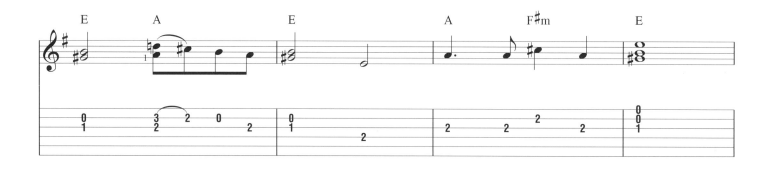

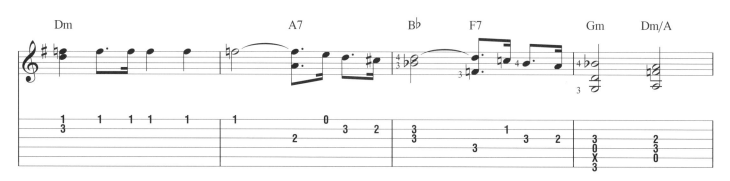

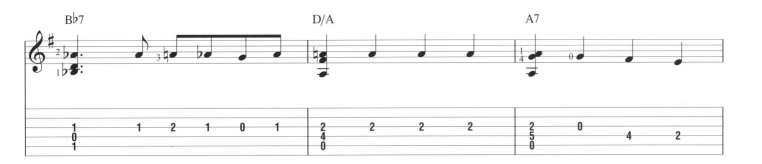

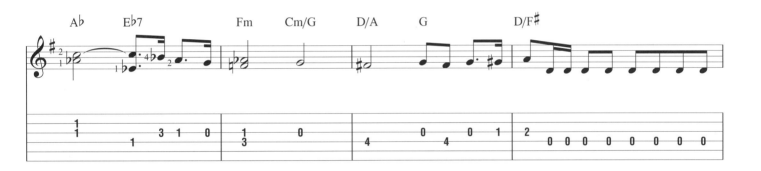

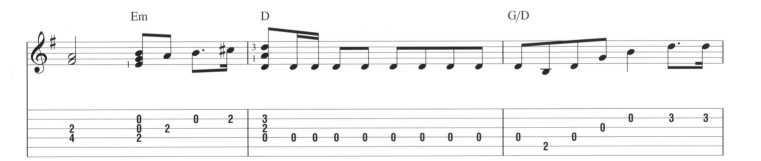

2nd time, D.C. al Fine

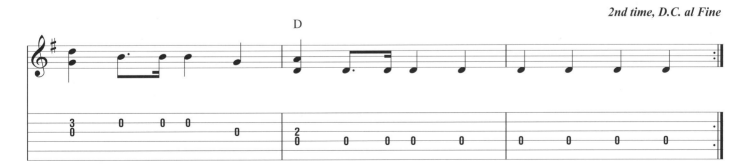

Minuet in F Major, K. 2

By Wolfgang Amadeus Mozart

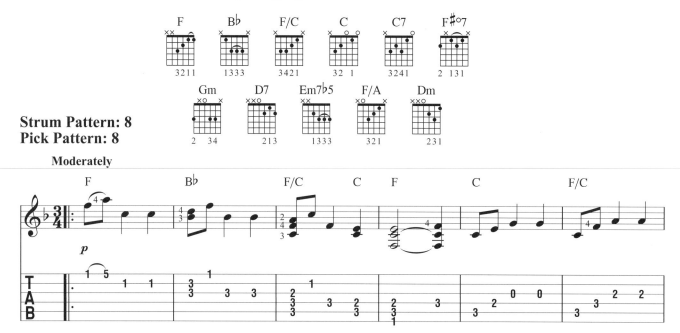

Strum Pattern: 8
Pick Pattern: 8

Moderately

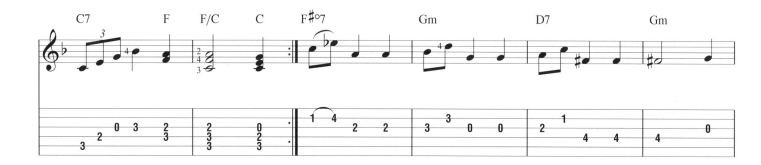

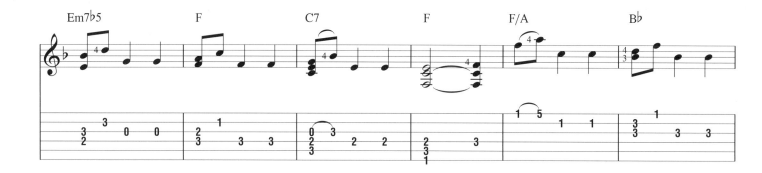

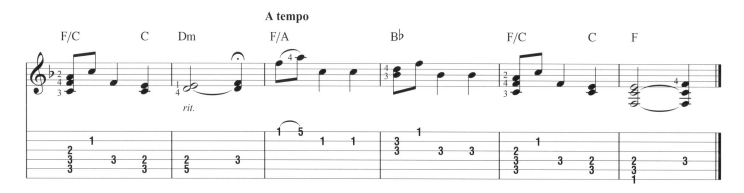

Piano Sonata in A

By Wolfgang Amadeus Mozart

Strum Pattern: 8
Pick Pattern: 8

Moderately

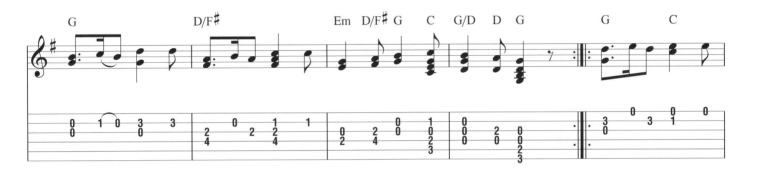

*Arranged in G major for playability.

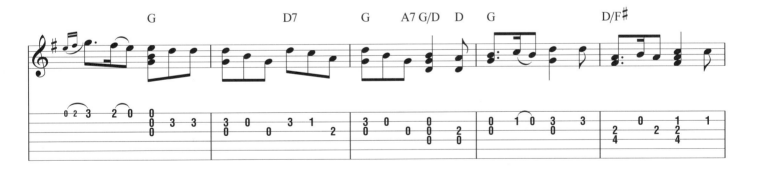

Morning

from PEER GYNT

By Edvard Grieg

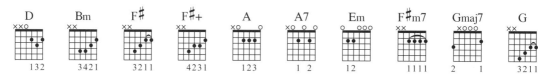

Strum Pattern: 8
Pick Pattern: 8

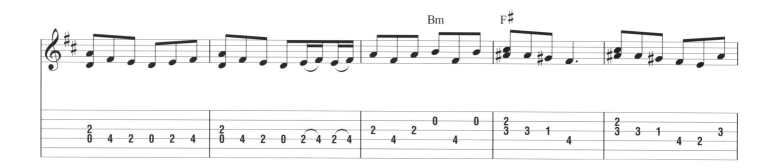

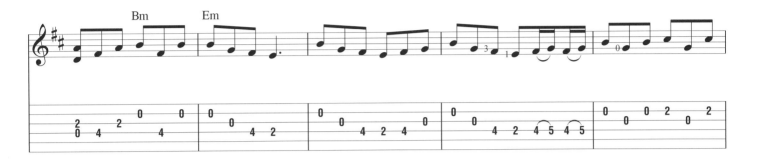

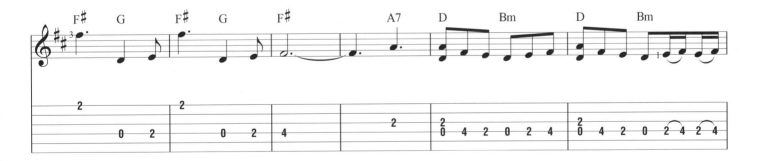

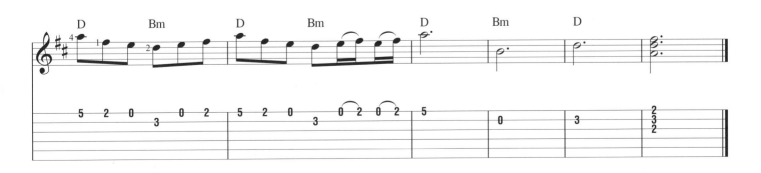

Piano Concerto in C

By Wolfgang Amadeus Mozart

Strum Pattern: 5
Pick Pattern: 5

Moderately slow

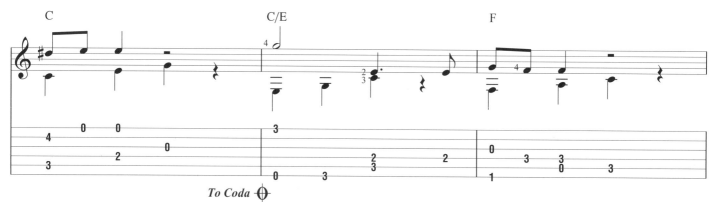

To Coda ⊕

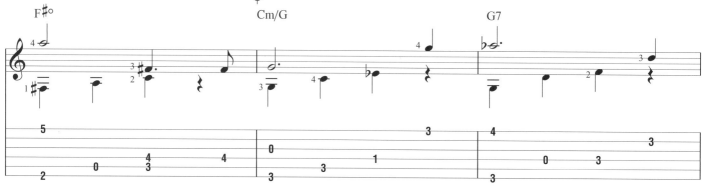

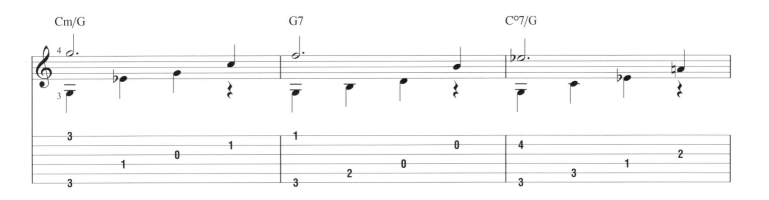

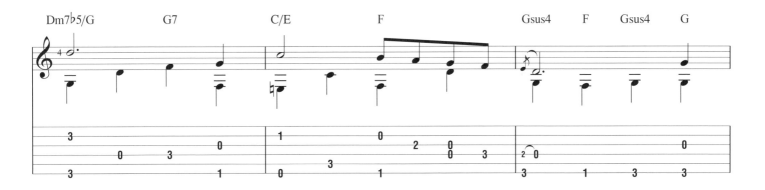

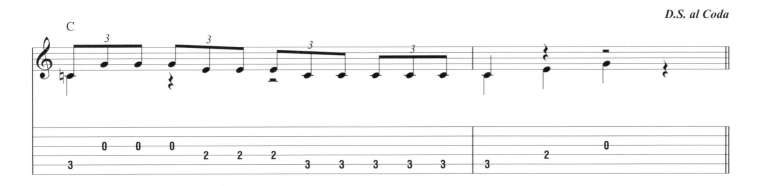

D.S. al Coda

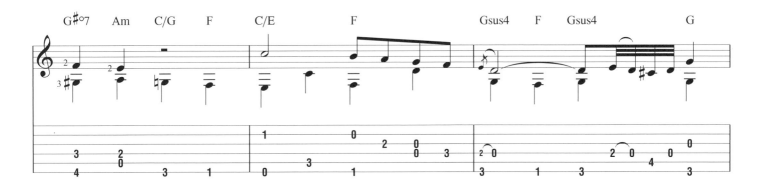

⊕ Coda

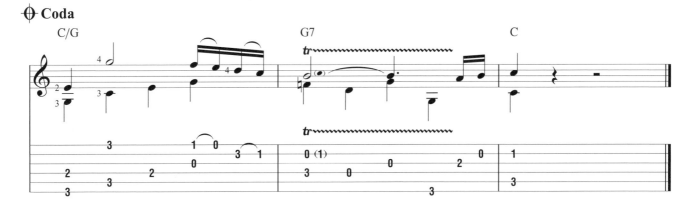

Prelude in C Minor, Op. 28, No. 20

By Fryderyk Chopin

Strum Pattern: 5
Pick Pattern: 1

Very slow

*Arranged in E minor for playability.

Sonatina in C Major, Op. 36, No. 1

By Muzio Clementi

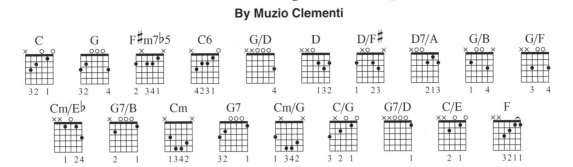

Strum Pattern: 3
Pick Pattern: 3

Intro
   Moderately, in 2

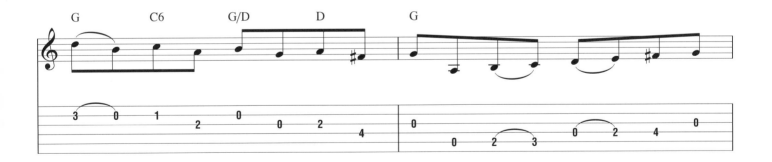

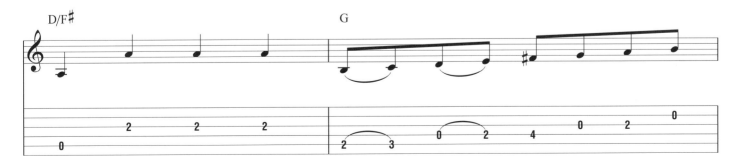

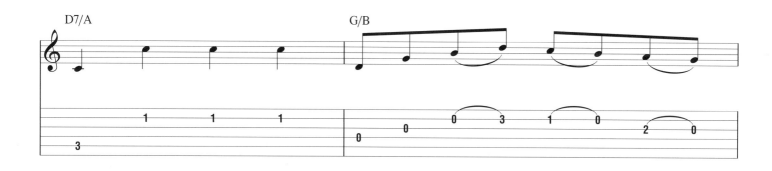

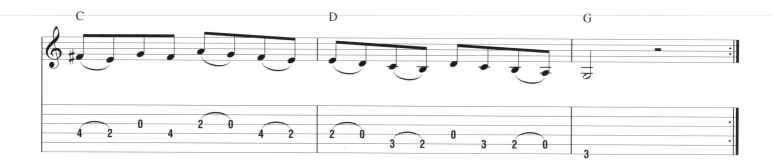

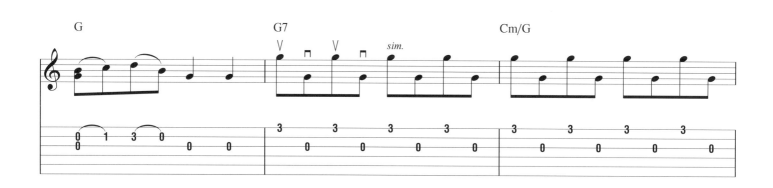

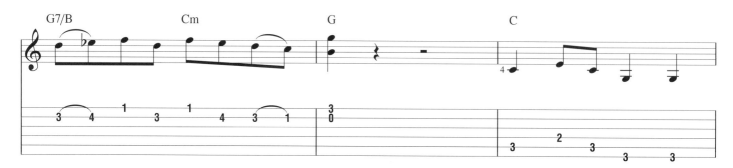

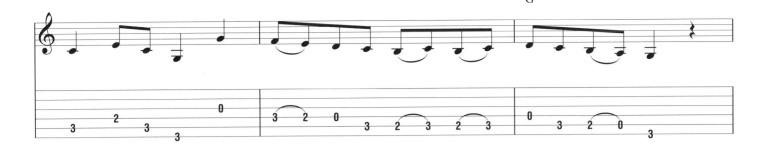

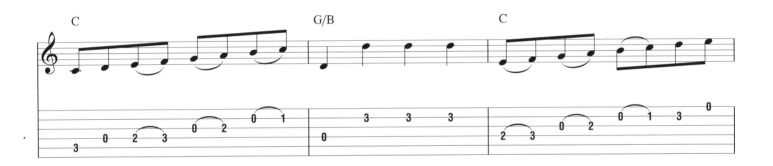

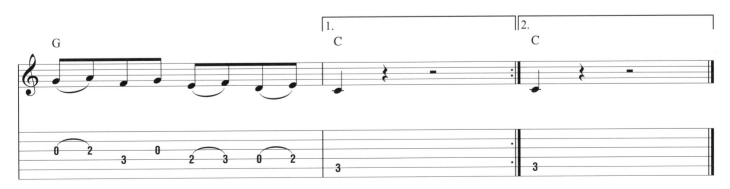

Romeo and Juliet (Love Theme)

By Pyotr Il'yich Tchaikovsky

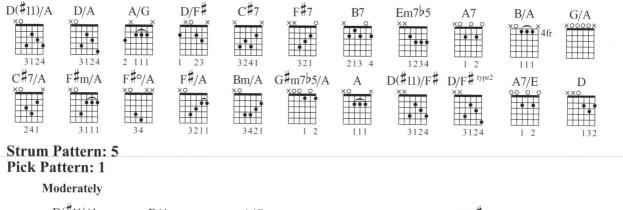

Strum Pattern: 5
Pick Pattern: 1

Moderately

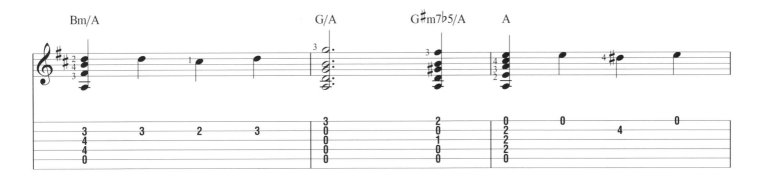

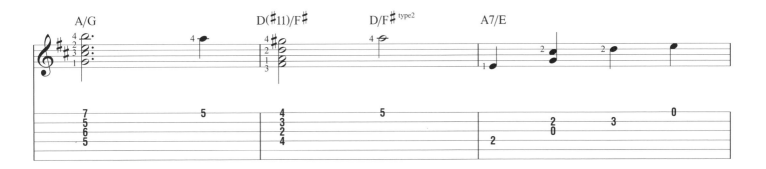

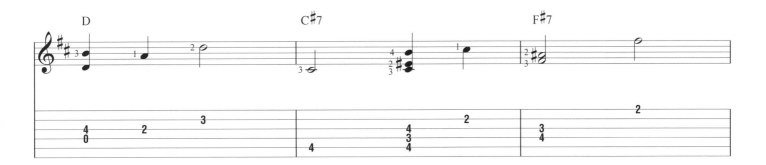

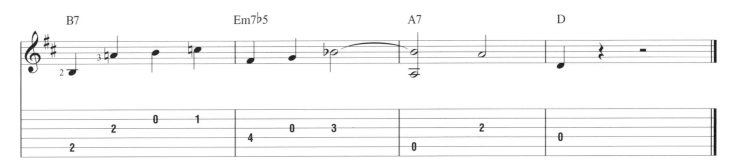

Rondeau

By Jean-Joseph Mouret

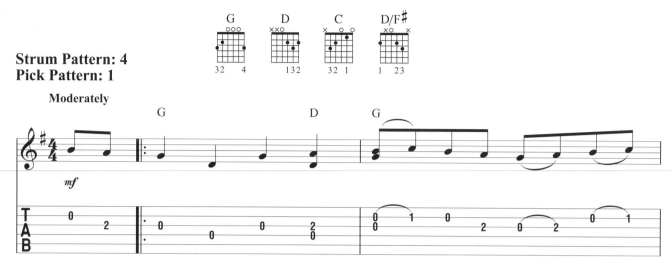

Strum Pattern: 4
Pick Pattern: 1

Moderately

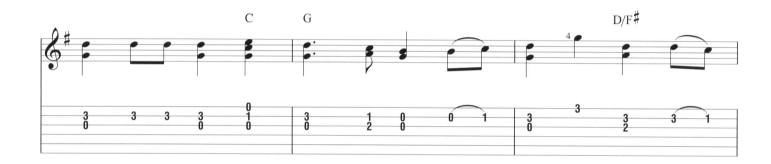

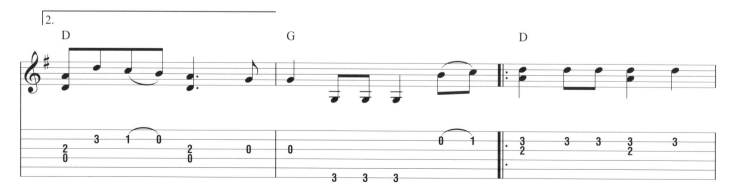

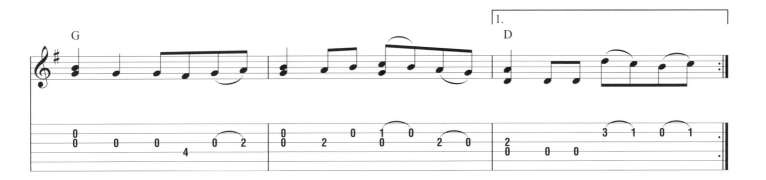

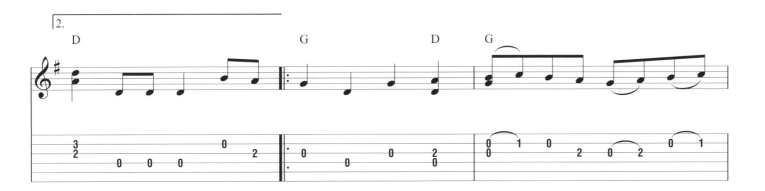

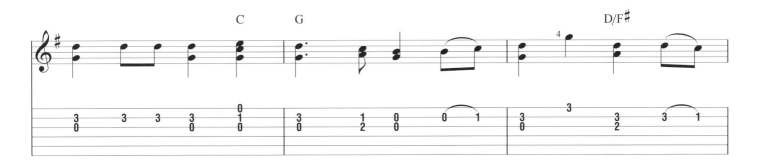

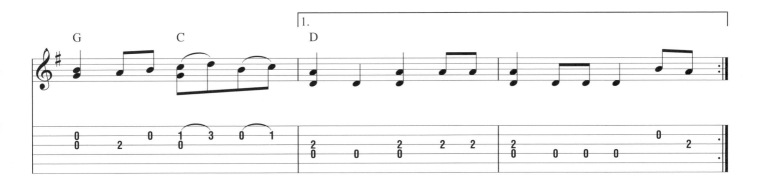

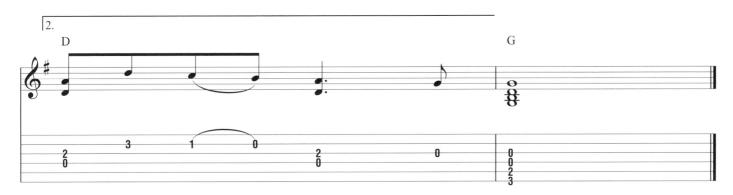

Sicilienne

By Gabriel Fauré

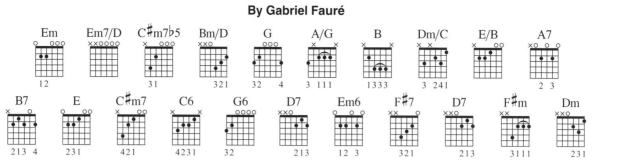

Strum Pattern: 8
Pick Pattern: 8

Slow, in 2

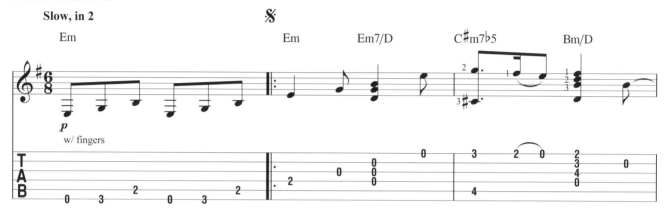

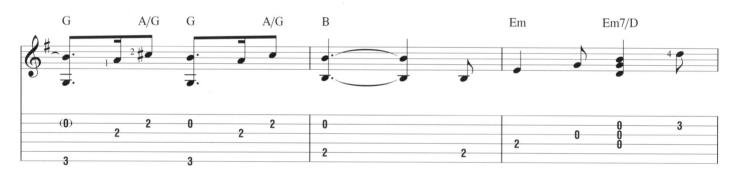

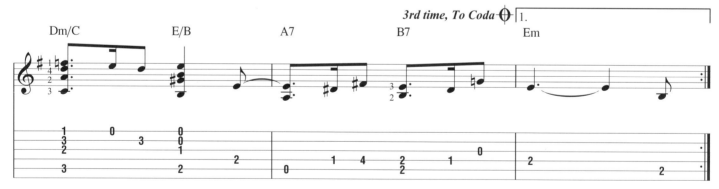

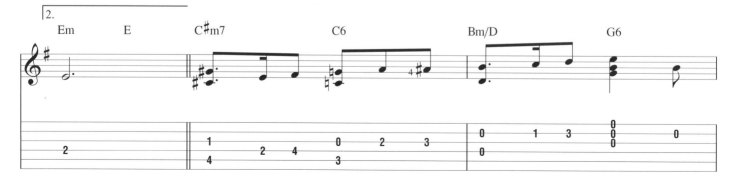

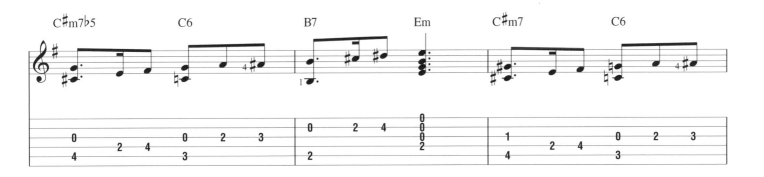

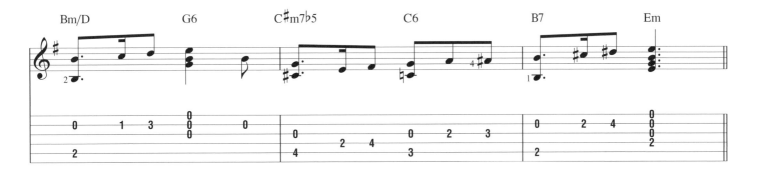

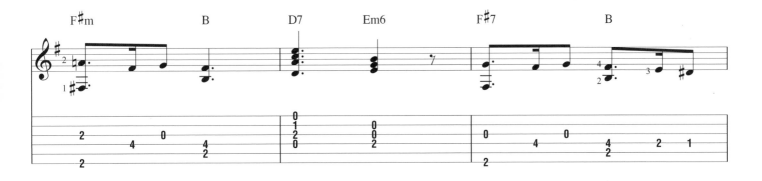

D.S. al Coda   Coda

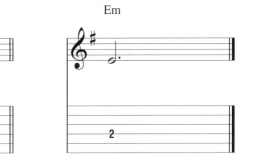

Spring Song, Op. 62, No. 6

from SONGS WITHOUT WORDS

By Felix Mendelssohn

Strum Pattern: 10
Pick Pattern: 10

Moderately slow

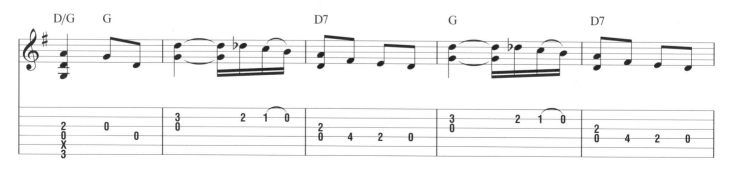

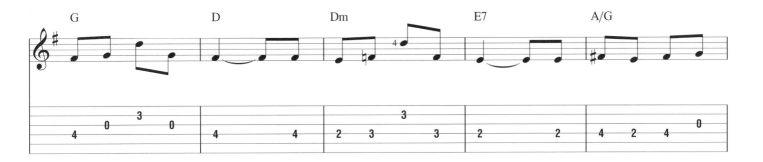

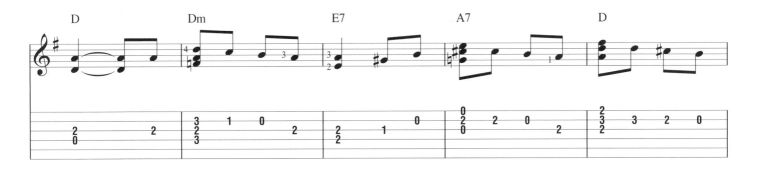

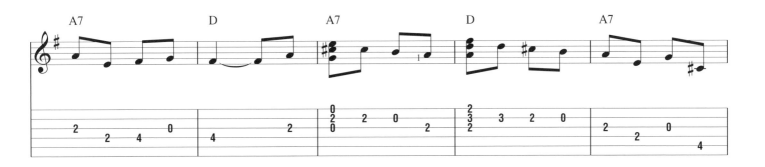

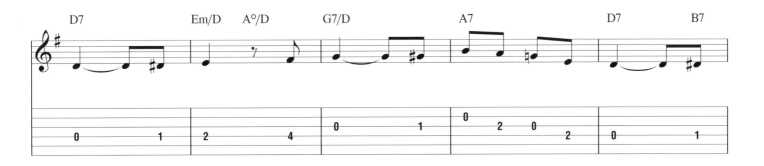

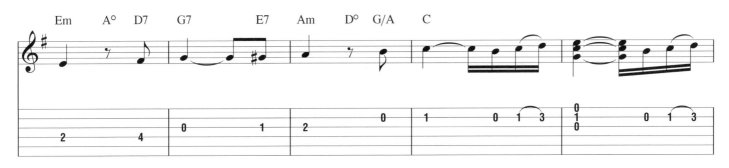

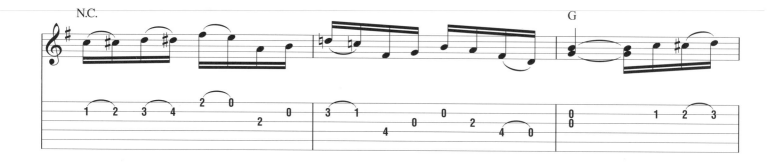

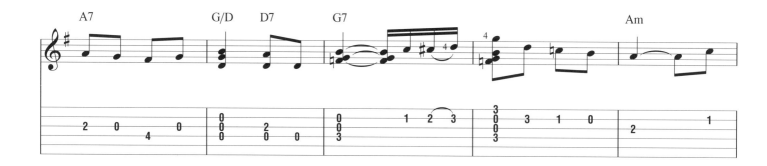

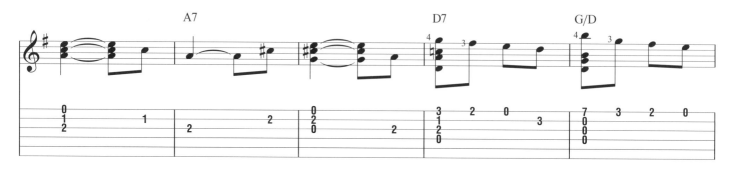

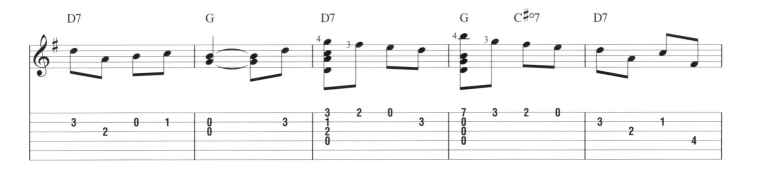

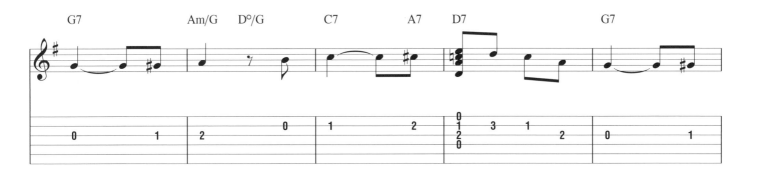

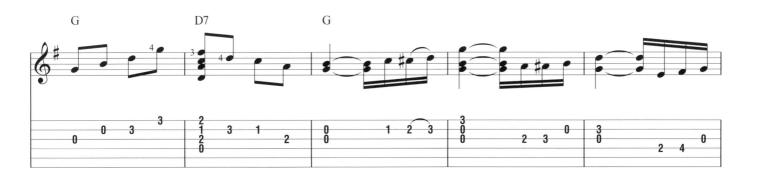

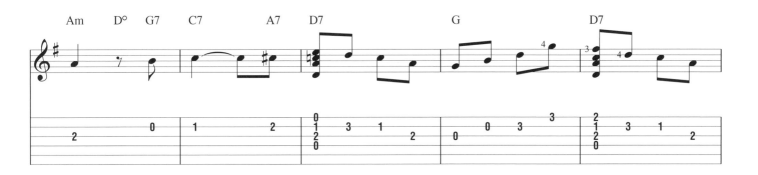

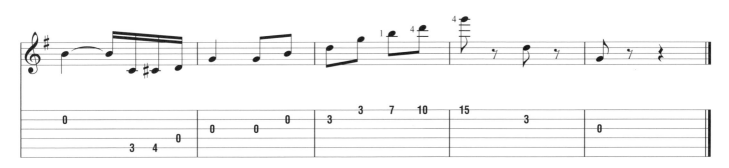

The Surprise Symphony

By Franz Joseph Haydn

C   F   G   D7   G7   F6

Strum Pattern: 10
Pick Pattern: 10

Intro
Moderately slow

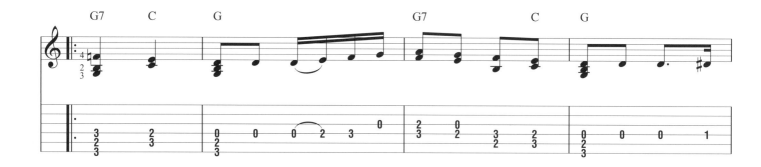

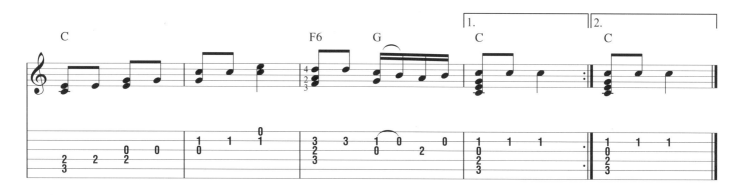

Trumpet Tune

By Henry Purcell

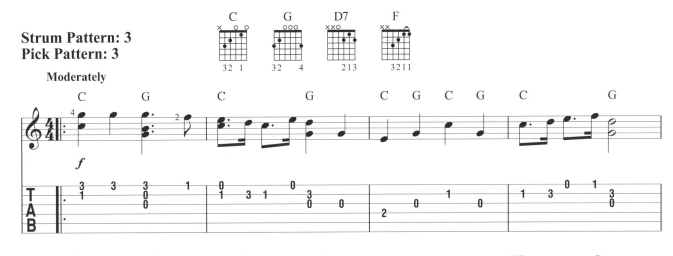

Strum Pattern: 3
Pick Pattern: 3

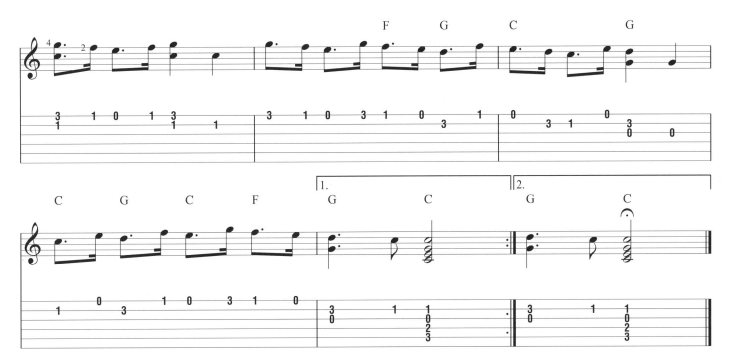

Toccata and Fugue in D Minor

By Johann Sebastian Bach

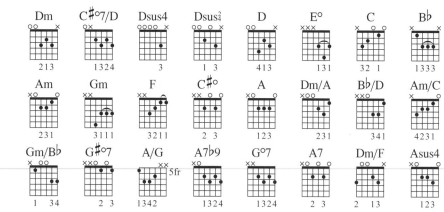

Drop D tuning:
(low to high) D-A-D-G-B-E

Freely

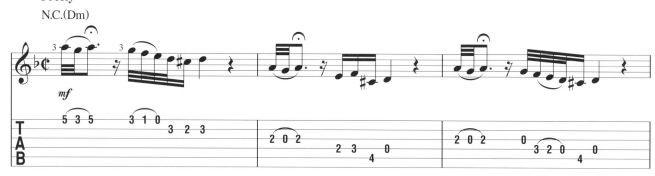

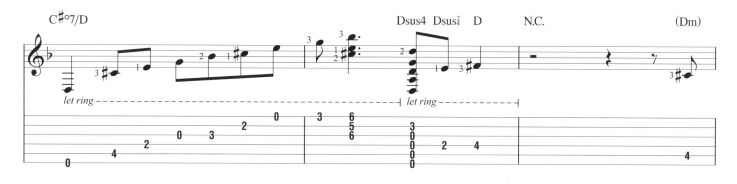

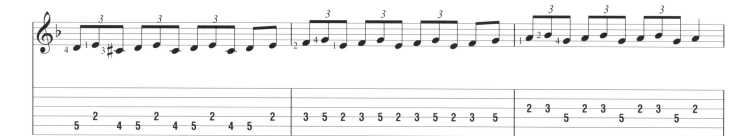

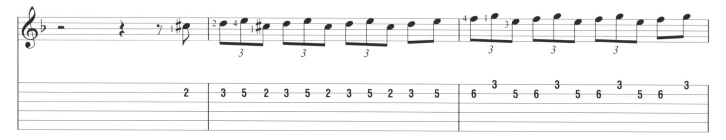

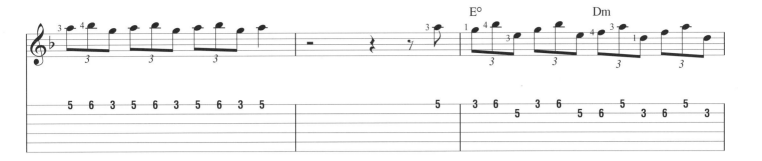

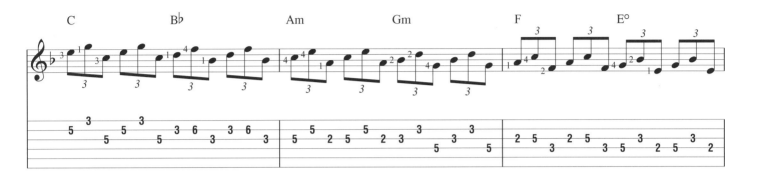

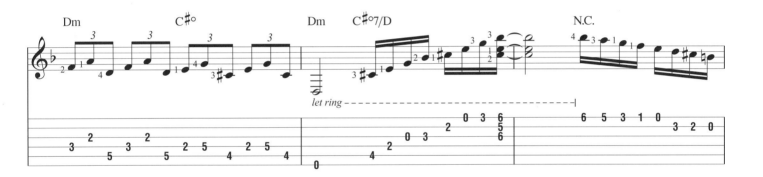

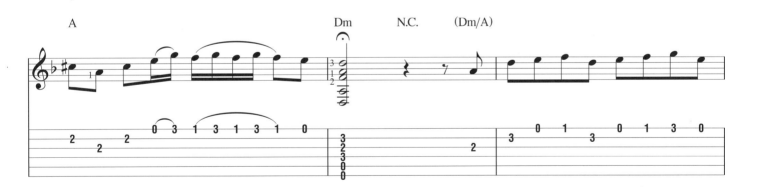

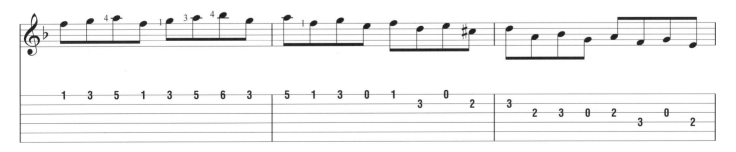

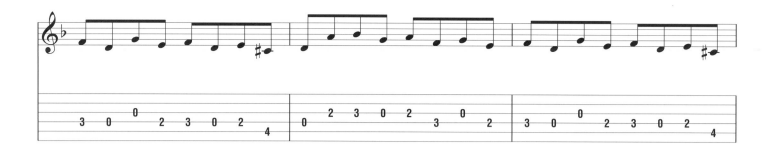

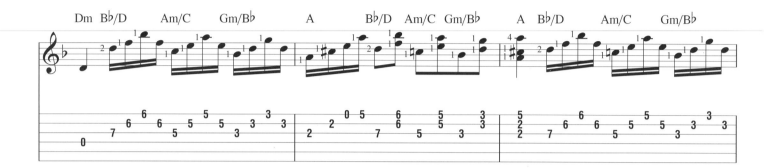

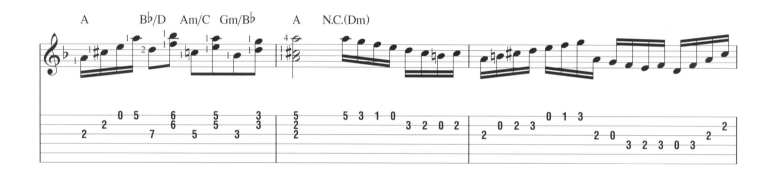

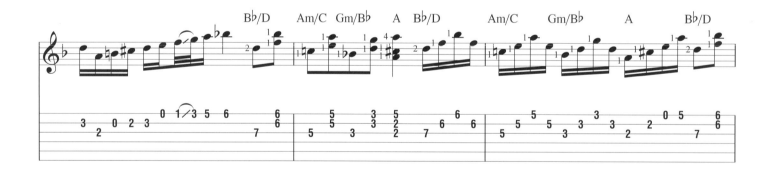

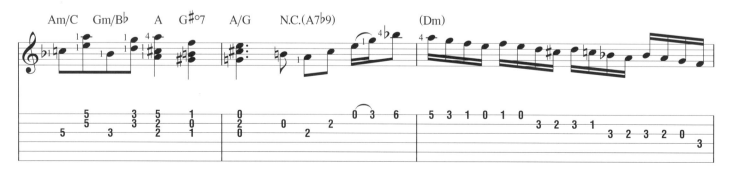

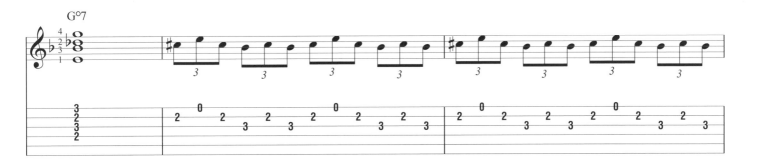

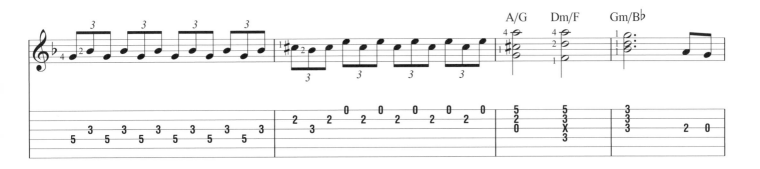

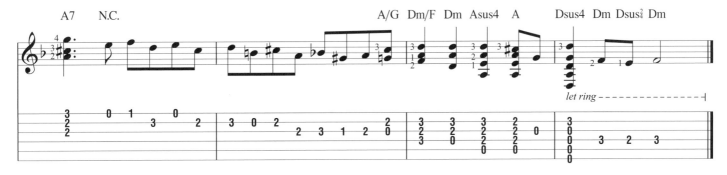

Toreador Song

from CARMEN

By Georges Bizet

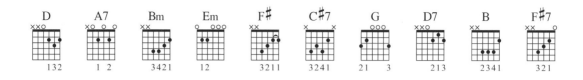

Strum Pattern: 4
Pick Pattern: 3

Moderately slow

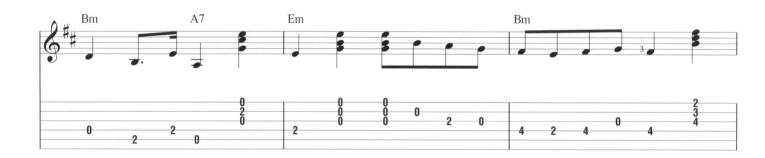

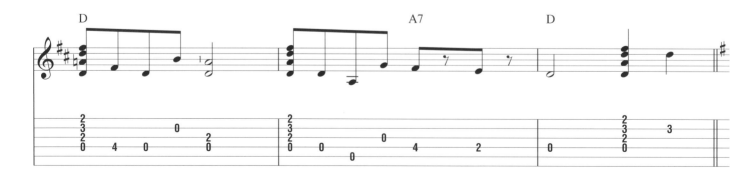

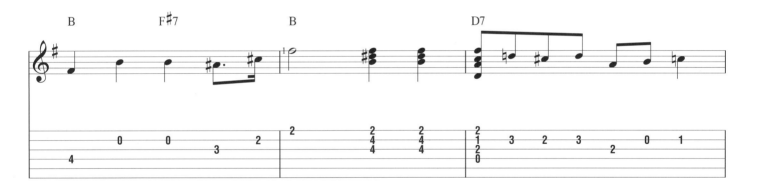

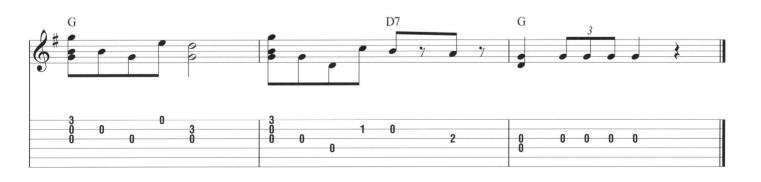

Trumpet Voluntary

By Jeremiah Clarke

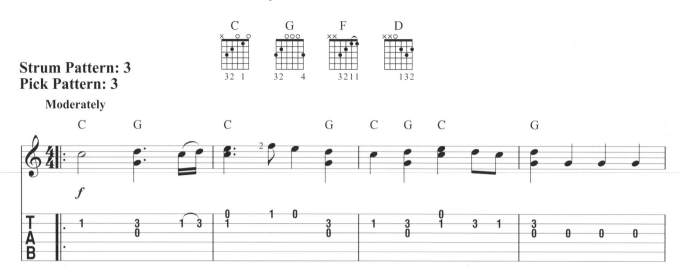

Strum Pattern: 3
Pick Pattern: 3

Moderately

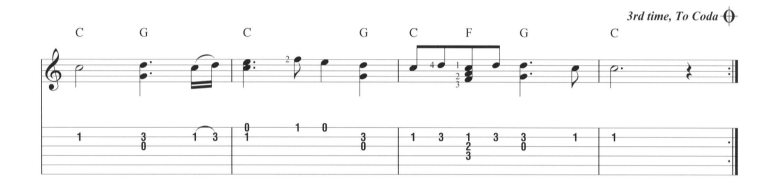

3rd time, To Coda ✛

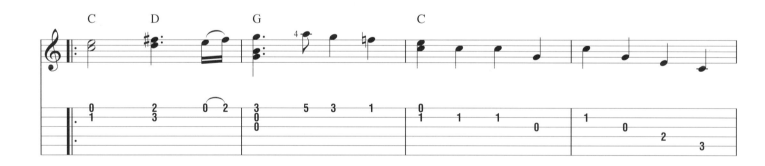

2nd time, D.C. al Coda
(no repeat)

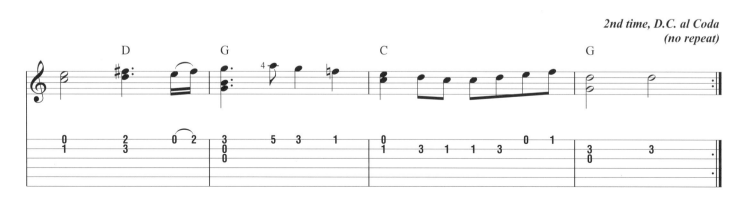

Coda

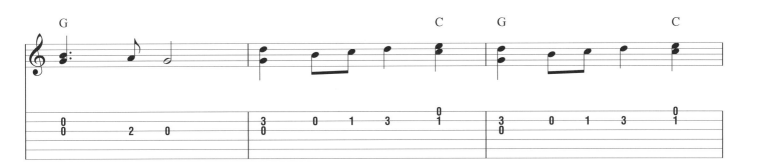

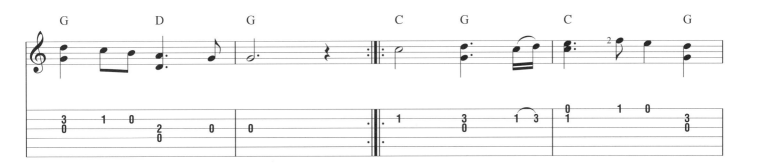

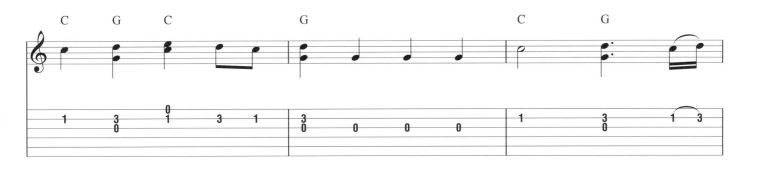

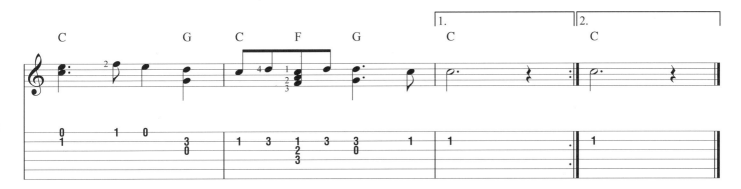

Turkish Rondo

from SONATA IN A MAJOR, K. 331, THIRD MOVEMENT EXCERPT

By Wolfgang Amadeus Mozart

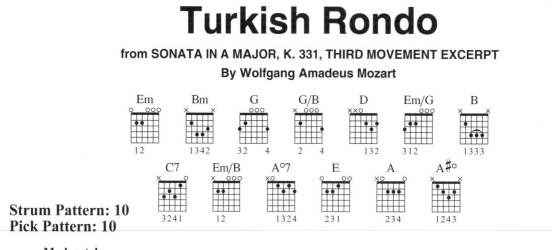

Strum Pattern: 10
Pick Pattern: 10

Moderately

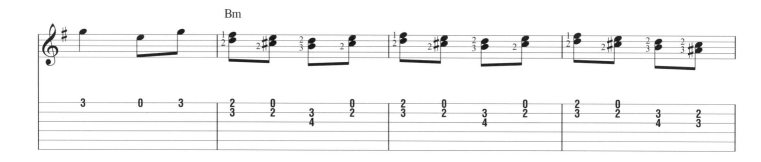

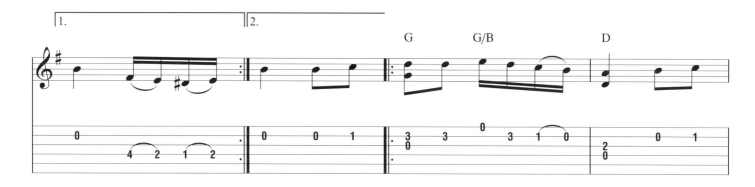

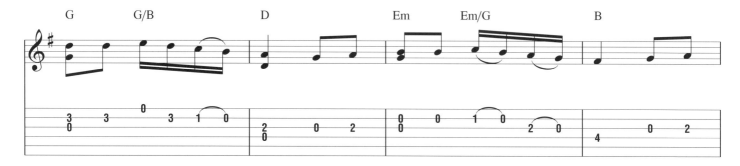

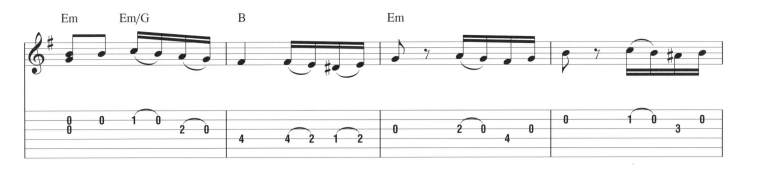

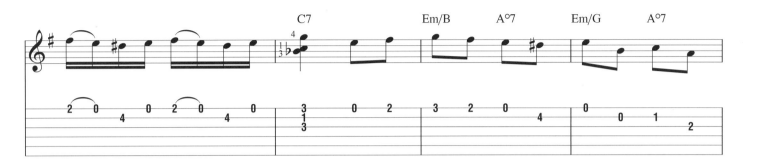

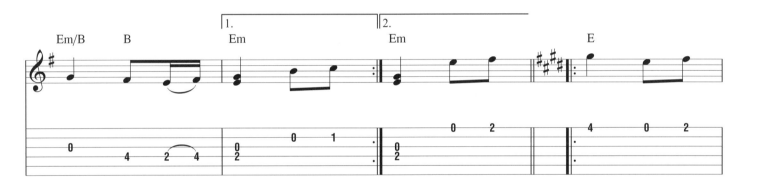

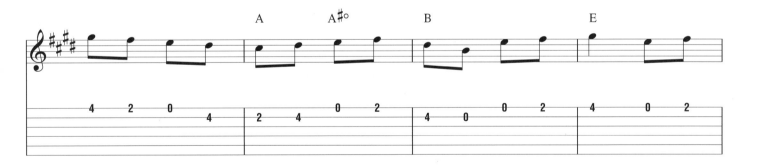

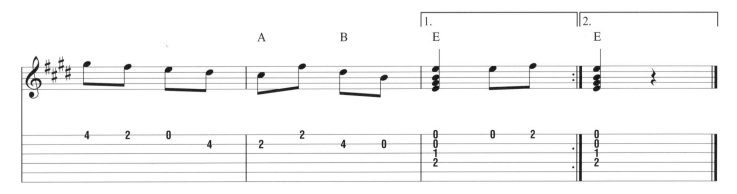

Una Furtiva Lagrima

from L'ELISIR D'AMORE (THE ELIXIR OF LOVE)

By Gaetano Donizetti

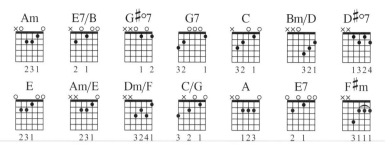

Strum Pattern: 8
Pick Pattern: 8

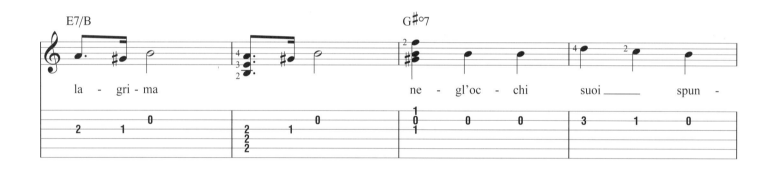

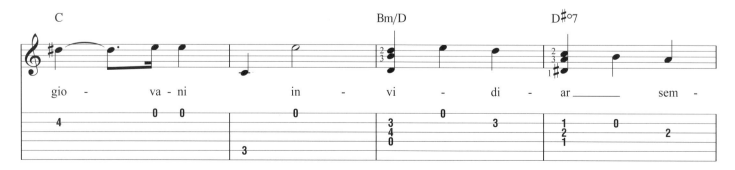

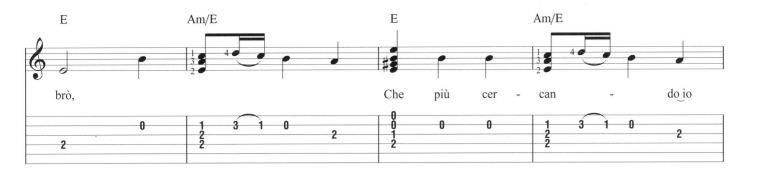

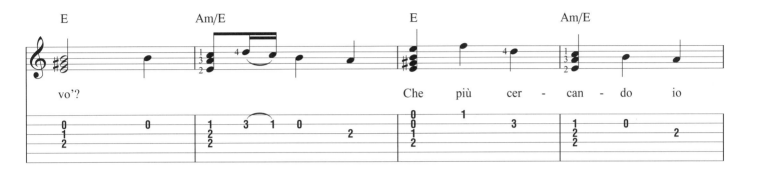

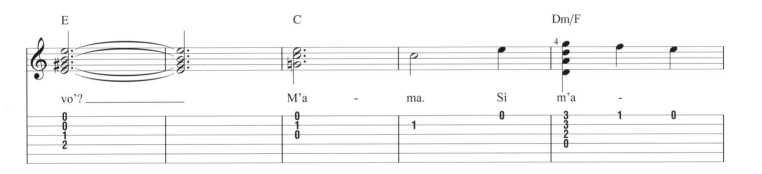

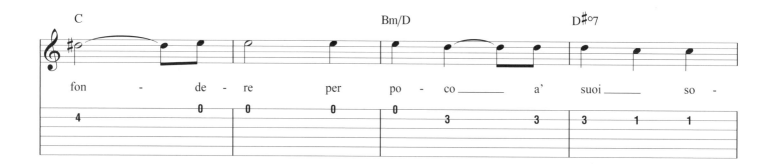

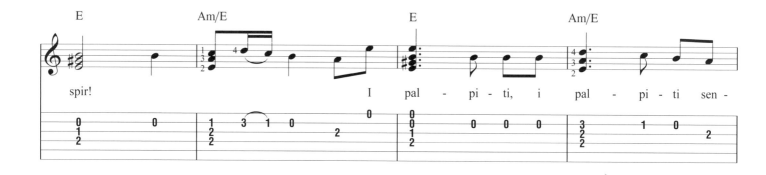

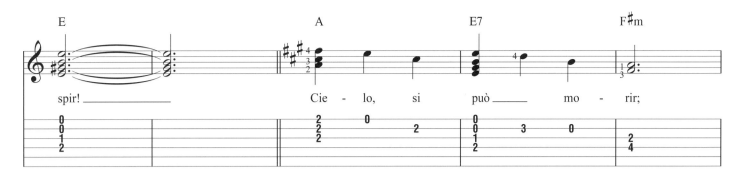

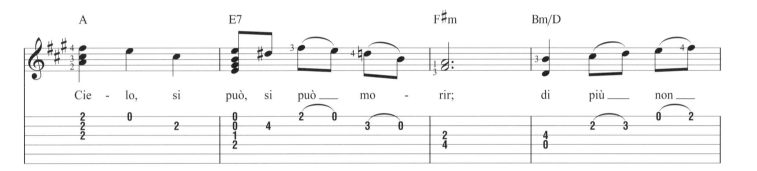

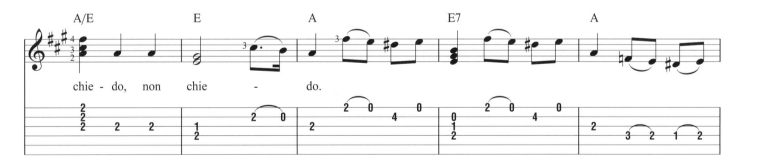

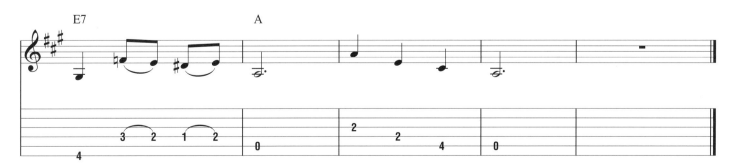

Waltz of the Flowers

from THE NUTCRACKER

By Pyotr Il'yich Tchaikovsky

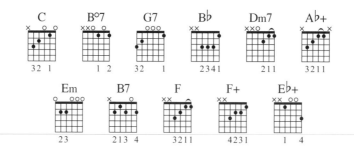

Strum Pattern: 8
Pick Pattern: 8

Moderately

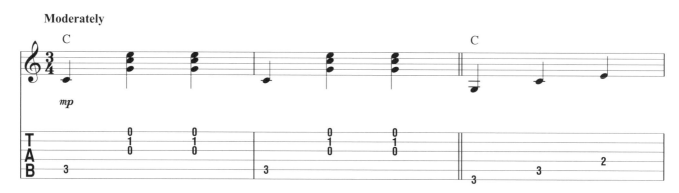

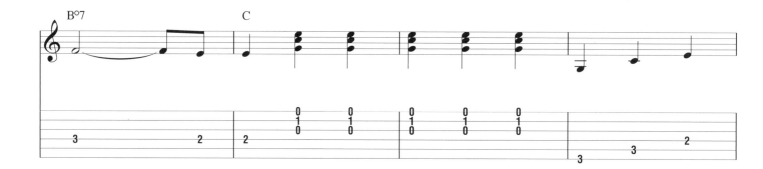

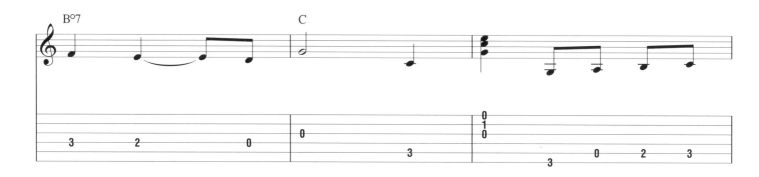

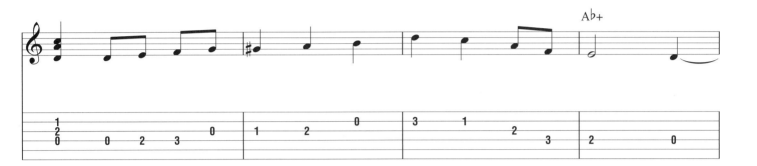

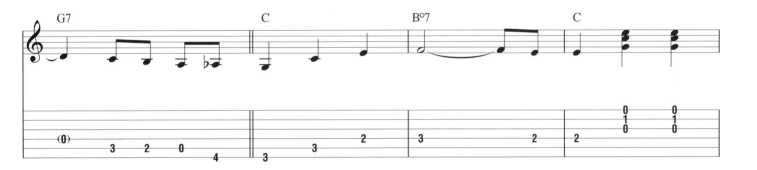

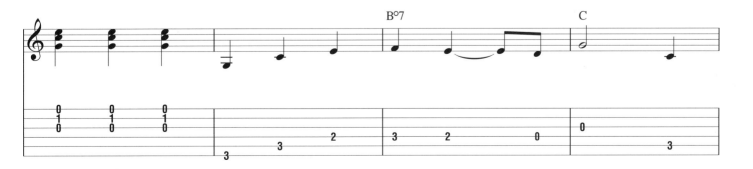

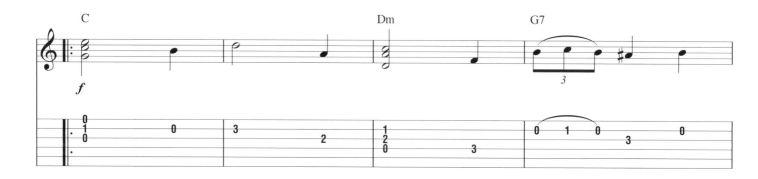

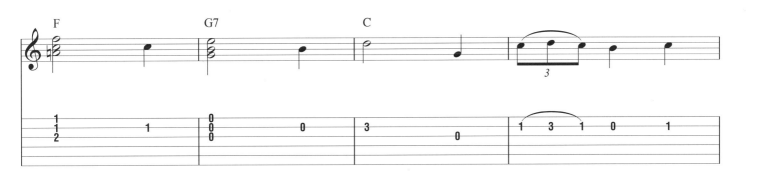

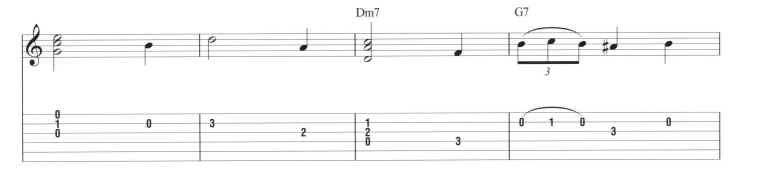

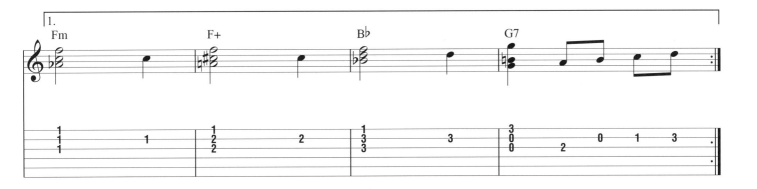

Wedding March

from A MIDSUMMER NIGHT'S DREAM

By Felix Mendelssohn

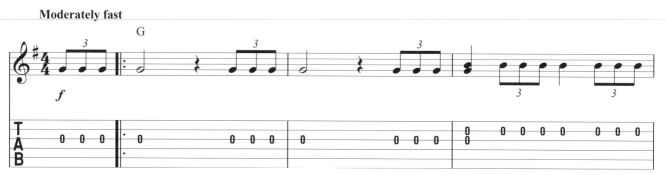

Strum Pattern: 3
Pick Pattern: 3

Moderately fast

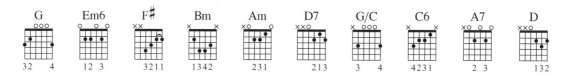

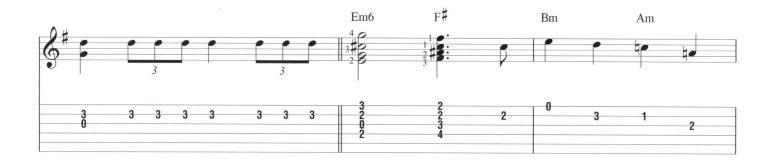

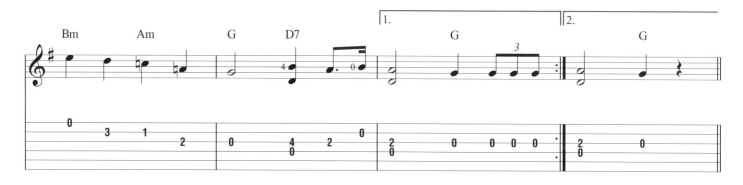

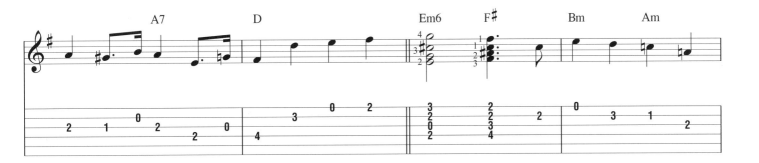

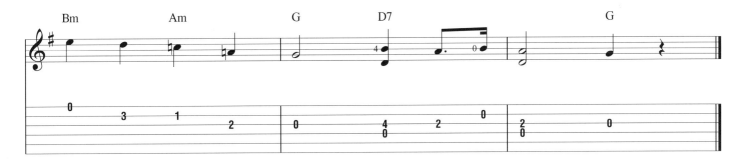

77

Voices of Spring

By Johann Strauss, Jr.

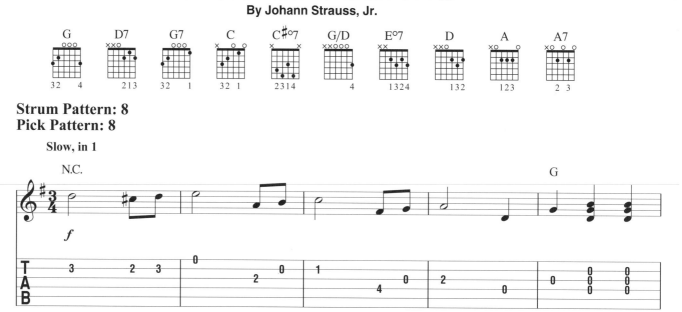

Strum Pattern: 8
Pick Pattern: 8

Slow, in 1

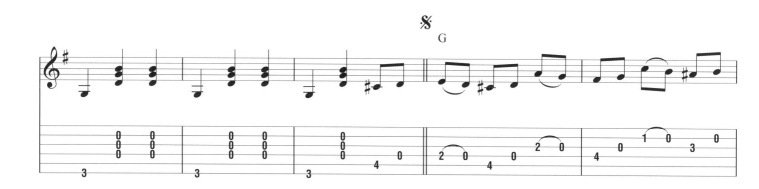

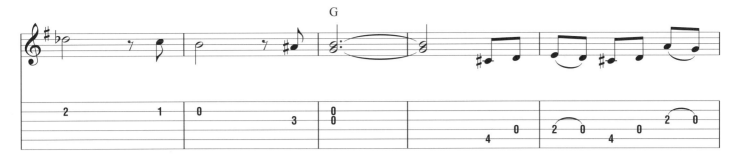

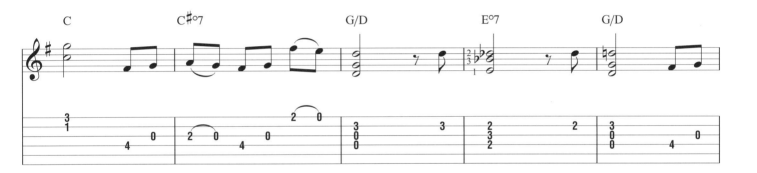

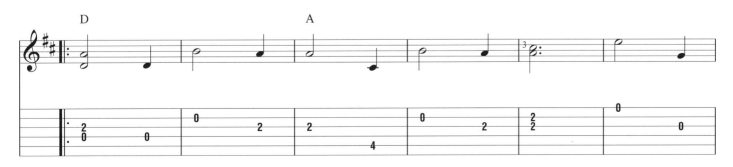

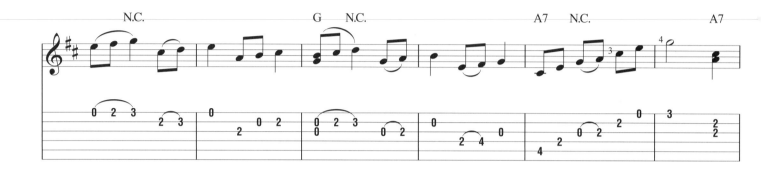

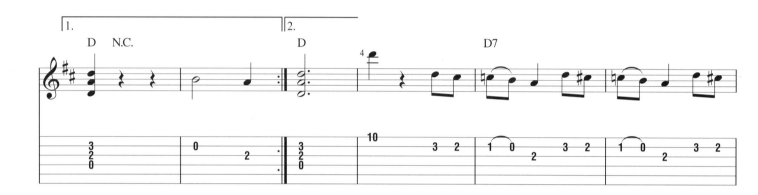

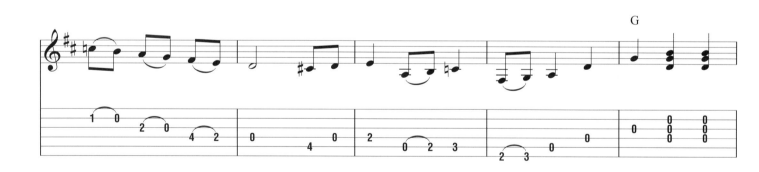